This book is to be returned on or before
the last date ~~~~~ below.

D1643656

Edward Hart

SHIRE HORSES

B.T. Batsford Ltd · London

ISBN 0 7134 4049 X

Filmset by Servis Filmsetting Ltd, Manchester
and printed in Great Britain by
The Anchor Press Ltd
Tiptree, Essex
for the publishers
B.T. Batsford Ltd
4 Fitzhardinge Street
London W1H 0AH

Frontispiece The Courage
Shire Horse Centre at
Maidenhead, Berkshire. The
premises are open to the
public for much of the year,
and include a farrier's shop
and souvenir shop. In its first
six years, 900,000 visitors
came to the Centre. Courage
Shires have taken part in the
Heavy Horse Musical Drive
at the Horse of the Year
Show ever since its inception
in 1951. The team has also
visited Holland

CONTENTS

ACKNOWLEDGMENT

My thanks go to: Bryan Holden, Abergele Heavy Horse Society; the Courage Shire Horse Centre; Daniel Thwaites Brewery, Blackburn; Devon Shire Horse Centre; Young's Brewery; Charlie Pinney; John Thompson and Lee Weatherley, for encouragement and photographs. I am also grateful to Roy Bird M.B.E., Tonie Gibson and staff of the Shire Horse Society, Peterborough; to Ike Bay and Arlin Wareing for photographs and information from the USA; to John Porter for reading the proofs and making available his books, records and extensive knowledge of pedigrees; to the brewery horsemen who have regaled us far into the night with their own product and great experience of heavy horses; to my wife Audrey for being a 'Shire widow' on occasion, for photographs, and for preparing the index so well; to Gillian Scott for typing the manuscript. Unless otherwise stated in the captions, the illustrations are from my own collection.

INTRODUCTION

The world of the Shire horse has many facets. The Shire remains the pride of English-speaking nations in an era when so much national confidence has been lost. The word itself conjures up visions of Midland counties in the heart of England where fertile soil grows leafy hedges, shady trees and huge crops.

The breed needs such conditions to thrive. The leading Shire studs are not, and never were, found high on the wet and windy Pennines, Snowdonia or Exmoor. So large an animal has a large capacity for food and, if this is not supplied in abundance, the great horse is not so useful as a strong pony that could subsist on less.

For each of us, the Shire horse has a personal meaning. For some it may represent a plough team pulling over the brow of a hill; for others, the more glamorous activity of hauling a brightly painted dray in show ring or city street. Yet a third group thinks first of the senior stallion class at Peterborough, or the grand parade there, a fitting finale to a day of Shires.

Some spend hours pouring over old prints, photographs and records of this great breed. The dark maroon outlines of stud books fill several shelves, one focal point in a room of Shire mementoes, stud cards and paintings. Even the spines of the books are a record of the breed, starting with comparatively slim volumes, thickening to over 1,100 pages in 1889 and 1890, with every pedigree beautifully spaced.

Other enthusiasts have developed the hobbies of model making and horse brass collecting. Each fancy now has its own society, with plans available for a host of waggons, carts and drays. A Shire is often the horse chosen in miniature to set off the vehicles.

Horse brass collectors can amass tasteful sets without great expense. And most things connected with the Shire appreciate with age, including the numerous designs in porcelain and metal. Nor do they incur running costs. For, as Mr Jorrocks said, 'Confound all presents wot eats!' – and the live Shire does eat a great deal.

This brings us to the horsemen themselves, who turn out night and morning to see to their charges, feed them with oats and sweet hay redolent of high summer, muck them out and bed them down with rustling, clean straw. They bring the real Shire atmosphere to the big shows. Brood mares tethered to waggons under the shade of big trees whicker at their foals, stallions stamp, bay yearlings whinney at every passing horse, grooms polish harness and chat.

Edward Thomas was doubtless thinking of Shires when he wrote:

. . . There was no sound but one.
Three cart-horses were looking over a gate
Drowsily through their forelocks, swishing their tails
Against a fly, a solitary fly.

1 A Shire mare and foal at the Devon Shire Horse Farm Centre. Few animals are more attractive to children – or anyone else – than a Shire foal. (*Western Morning News Co. Ltd*)

To those of us brought up with them, the sight, sound and sweat of Shires returning to summer stable will never be forgotten. The rubbing of the great heads against our shoulder – more from convenience than affinity! – and the smell of leather saddles being slung up to dry became part of our being. Then they seemed lost, but now they are with us again.

Yet another source of pleasure in which the Shire has played its part is the resurgence of heavy-horse literature. Unbelievably, more books have been written on the heavy horse since 1970 than in the whole preceding time. Many of these new ones are magnificently produced, with informative black and white photographs and attractive colour ones.

Today the Shire establishes a bond between mankind as never before. It

2 Roy and Prince ploughing at the Devon Shire Horse Farm Centre, where in 1981 20 Shires were kept, six of them in-foal mares (*Western Morning News Co. Ltd*)

joins Suffolk, Clydesdale, Percheron, Belgian and Ardennes fanciers in a worldwide brotherhood. Fortunately, the days when a Shire man referred to rival breeds as 'the enemy' have passed.

King and commoner were linked by the Shire in the heady days of King Edward VII, who was followed by his son King George V, a great Shire breeder. Today the head of a huge company and the groom of a small stable have a mutual interest and respect, all engendered by the Shire.

3   Three of the Courage Shires. Post-and-rails make the best fencing for horses; wire, especially if barbed, can be dangerous. Natural materials are also better for such items as hay nets; synthetics and livestock do not mix. (*Walton Adams*)

4   What a grand foal! Each succeeding year among the Shires becomes more interesting, with the delight in seeing how last season's foals have fared, and which mares are breeding to which stallions (*Audrey Hart*)

1 In the Beginning

The Great Horse

From the record of the Roman historian Tacitus we know that Queen Boadicea's Britons used horses to draw their chariots. There seems no evidence, however, that these were any bigger than strong ponies.

The Great Horse, or War Horse, came later. While only the culls were left for farming, the English knights rode stallions, and only stallions capable of carrying up to four hundredweight. A short-coupled, deep ribbed animal was needed for this weight, something well above Fell pony size, which at 14 hands maximum carried lead on panniers, eight stone a side and 240 miles a week.

The armoured knight did not need a horse to carry him such a distance, but he did need one to take his weight and to manoeuvre actively as well. Belonging to the affluent minority, he would be proud enough to seek an exceptional animal, and able to pay for it when he found it. That the horse's back was short is indicated from early prints, pictures and plates in which the saddle reached almost from the withers to the croup.

The heyday of the Great Horse as mount for armoured knights was from the Norman invasion of 1066 to the Battle of Bannockburn in 1314. William the Conqueror's army of horsemen triumphed over the English army of foot soldiers led by Harold. But they did not ride heavies. From the Bayeux tapestry, 14 hands seems to have been the maximum height.

The horses that came over with the Normans certainly helped to lay the foundations of the Old English breed of cart horses. From a book written c.1154, we find that 'Cart Horses fit for the dray, the plough, or the chariot' were on sale at Smithfield, London, every Friday.

Just as the Clydesdale was founded on a stout and active type of native horse, top-crossed with Great Horse stallions, so we may reasonably assume that the Normans' stallions were put onto sound native horses of the type that once drew chariots. Then, during the reign of King John (1199–1216), 100 stallions of 'large stature' were imported from the Low Countries.

Scotland enters the story at Bannockburn. King Robert the Bruce rode a 'palfrey' that took heavy toll of the more ponderous English heavies, and afterwards the knights began to look for something faster and more nimble. Another effect was that stallions left behind by the English were put to use on Scottish mares, further helping to found the Clydesdale which by 1823 had a class devoted to it at the Highland Society's Show. This was 60 years before the Shire gained similar recognition at the English Royal (see page 25).

We may imagine the pangs of regret that accompanied the Great Horse's decline. The change to a lighter type of galloping horse, so effectively used by

5 Cart horse 1808. Here is no mean draught animal. It lacks the feather of a century later, and has a finer face and ears, but the bone is substantial, and the length of tail interesting. The horse is obviously well kept

6 Scotch farm horse. Undated print, but the face and curved, pointed ears are similar to the cart horse (shown in fig. 5). The Scotch collar has a slight peak; high peaks appeared later. The horse has a slight amount of feather and is decorated, possibly for a ploughing match

Cromwell's Roundheads in the Civil War, must have caused heartaches similar to those experienced by lovers of the heavy horse in the 1950s. There is no evidence of such a dramatic change after 1314, however; things moved more slowly then, and far fewer numbers were involved.

All our modern heavy breeds are derived from the Great Horse of Europe, in its turn descended from the so-called 'cold-blooded' horses of Central Europe.

Horse Breeding

In Tudor and Stuart times, horse breeding schemes were largely the prerogative of the squire, the sportsman and the soldier. Tenant farmers appear to have used what mares they had, with the stallions which were to hand. The days when Shire horse breeding became a ruling passion in men's lives, even a reason for farming rather than purely a means of providing power, were far ahead.

Yet the agricultural horse had a vital role to play in the farm's economy. A large number of horses were needed both for road transport and the army, and most of the former were farm-bred. Just as in later times of agricultural depression the breeding of Shires for town use kept many a farming family on the land, so in the sixteenth and seventeenth centuries horse breeding was an important form of land use.

Draught Horses

Until the Middle Ages most of the heavy draught work in Britain was done by teams of oxen. Their use was general until the mid-eighteenth century, and even in 1794 George Culley of Northumberland was advancing lucid arguments in the oxen's favour.

But above all, the conclusion [between an ox fatted for the shambles, after working three or four years, or indeed a lean ox sold to feed, and a horse sold to the dog-kennel] is so exceedingly striking, that I presume most people, when they reflect upon this very important matter, will agree to the drawing of oxen in every kind of work wherein they *suit*. I advance this opinion on several years experience [employing about 150 oxen in the draught, on his and his brother's farms] but would recommend the oxen and horses be in separate draughts, because the difference of the step is so very unequal.

Ten years later his views appear to have modified. With J. Bailey he speaks of the heavy, rough-legged, black stallions which bred 'the draught-horses, which in general are middle-sized, active animals, well adapted to the husbandry of the country'.

The detailed figures that follow show that cost accounting is not a twentieth-century prerogative.

Three working horses, about $15\frac{1}{2}$ hands high, eat in 14 days 96 stones of hay, which is for each horse at the rate of 16 stones a week, with an allowance of oats, 12 gallons per week. Mr Jobson's, of Newton, 5 years old working oxen, with full allowance of hay, had, each ox, 6 quarts of oats per day. In 15 days 4 oxen eat 164 stones 7lb of hay, or $19\frac{1}{2}$ stones per ox per week.

Nor was there much to choose between the individual rations of horses and oxen when *not* at work.

An unworked ox, $3\frac{1}{2}$ years old, was put to good old meadow hay on the 29th of November, and eat 49 stones in 21 days; or, per week, 16 stones 5lb. An idle horse ($15\frac{1}{2}$ hands high) eat of the same hay 20 stones in 10 days; or, per week, 14 stones; had no corn.

The difference was in the number of animals required per team. At three years old, eight oxen are needed to do the work of two horses. A year later, 'having become tractable and stronger, 6 [oxen] are equal to 2 horses. Oxen, to work regularly through the year, cannot work more than half a day at a time'.

The Black Horse

Culley mentions four breeds of working horses, but not the Shire. Those listed are the Cleveland Bay, the Clydesdale, the Suffolk and the heavy Black horse.

The Blacks were bred almost universally through the Midland counties, particularly Leicestershire, Warwickshire, Staffordshire and Derbyshire, all great Shire strongholds today.

On the mares fell the full burden of both work and breeding. Apart from the stallions, all the males were sold.

These [the mares] are all put to the horse, the male produce of which supply the army, London, and most of the south and western counties, with horses for their farming-teams. The largest go to the capital for dray-horses; the next supply the farmers in the southern counties, for their waggons, ploughs etc. and the rest mount our cavalry, or are trained for carriages, while a few of the choicest are very properly preserved for stallions.

Culley cites an Earl of Huntingdon as returning from a Continental embassy with a set of 'coach horses of the black breed'. Most of these were stallions, and, probably with some difficulty, the Earl put pressure on his tenants by the Trent-side to use these Blacks on their mares. 'Which cross answered so well, that the breed in that neighbourhood has been in the greatest repute ever since,' said Culley.

Robert Bakewell

Robert Bakewell came across these horses, naturally enough, for he lived at Dishley Grange, Loughborough, Leicestershire, throughout his life from 1725 to 1795.

Bakewell is of interest to the story in three main ways. Firstly, he changed the Longhorn from a draught animal into an improved meat producer. Realizing that in the future cattle would be kept more for meat and milk than for power, he also concerned himself with improving the draught horse that would replace them; and finally, he instituted a system of hiring stallions.

Until Bakewell's day, horses had been used primarily for hunting, racing, coaching and military purposes. The potential of those Black horses around Trent-side impressed him so much that he and George Salisbury set out in search of stallions and mares with which to improve the English breed.

'After much labour and expense, they returned with half-a-dozen Dutch or Flanders mares,' says Culley. Bakewell embarked on a programme of continued selection and careful breeding. The distinctive type of draught horse evolved was in demand from the army as well as from farmers. He replaced the length, looseness of form and the long, thick, hairy legs of the old Blacks with a more compact, short-limbed and more active animal, which he claimed had a better constitution.

Yet time was overtaking even Bakewell, for though these Dutch mares were of use in improving the Leicester Black breed, demand for the latter was flagging. Culley remarks that the nobility and gentry had begun to run bay horses in their carriages, and light horses were more used in the army. Only for drays and waggons were the heavy Blacks in prime demand.

'The present [late eighteenth-century] system of farming requires horses of more mettle and activity, better adapted for travelling, and more capable of enduring fatigue,' writes Culley. He cites the Cleveland farmers of Yorkshire, and the Norfolk farmers, who plough from two to near three acres per day, with one pair of horses, 'a feat that would be impossible without a "hardier and nimbler breed than those alluded to" [the Blacks]'.

Robert Bakewell's system of hiring stallions has had vast repercussions on the heavy-horse industry. He did the same with sheep and cattle, though today the demand for hired bulls is small because of the widespread use of artificial insemination, and in sheep it is so far limited to breeders keen to assess the potential of a ram lamb.

In the heavy-horse world, the stallion hiring system can be claimed to be the very basis of improvement (see page 88). The highest price that Bakewell is known to have charged for a stallion is 150 guineas for the season, while home service fees were said to be 5 guineas.

Writing to George Culley of Northumberland on 8 December 1786, Bakewell offers to hire one of his horses:

If you think you and your friends would like to have him on the same terms as last year (viz.) Eighty Guineas, you bearing all expenses except me paying the Man's Wages. . . . Great Numbers of foles have been sold this Season from 8 to 12 in the cutting way and Yearling Colts and Fillies from 15 to 22; what more useful to pay rent than with this kind?

That is yet another example of how heavy horses were expected to play their part as saleable commodities. In modern times economists talk glibly about 'cash flow', yet every single form of mechanical power on the farm is an expense neither self-perpetuating nor appreciating in value.

By April 1792, Robert Bakewell was doing even better with his hirings:

I have the Pleasure to inform you the Horse and Bull Trades have been very good this Season. Last year, I had a horse in South Wales hired by a Gentleman for the use of his Tenants, and this Season I have one in North Wales to which they have entered into a Subscription for a Hundred mares at 2 Gs. and Half a Crown each Mare.

9 The harness on this Improved Black does not differ fundamentally from that used today. The shoes appear to be dished or concave

I wonder if the half-crown was for the groom? If so, it set a standard that remained unchanged right throughout the nineteenth century and up to World War Two. The old stud cards usually end, when stating fees, 'and half a crown for the groom'.

According to Thomas Dykes, horses bred by Bakewell contributed to the development of the heavier type of Clydesdale. In the *Transactions of the Highland Agricultural Society*, 1907, under the title 'Clydesdale Memories', he states that, not content with selling stallions into Scotland to the Duke of Buccleuch and other breeders, Bakewell sent north two Black horses of his own breeding. These were stationed alternately, three days a week at the Crown Hotel, Linlithgow, and for four days at quarters in the Edinburgh Grass Market. They were made much use of, and Black horse blood as distinct from old type Clydesdale came into general demand.

In the *Edinburgh Advertiser* of May, 1774, a Bakewell stallion known as Young Sampson is described, and 'is allowed to be the best black horse ever shown in Scotland'.

In 1795 Robert Bakewell died, having impoverished himself through his lavish hospitality at Dishley Grange. He had been made bankrupt in 1776, but recovered and passed on his herd and flock to his nephew, Robert Honeyborn.

Those who would emulate Bakewell's stock-breeding skill may be interested in his characteristics and routine. Prothero quotes a description:

A tall, broad-shouldered, stout man of brown-red complexion, clad in a loose brown coat and scarlet waistcoat, leather breeches and top boots. He adds that while entertaining in his kitchen Russian princes, French and German royal dukes, British peers, and sightseers of every degree, he never altered the routine of his daily life. Breakfast at eight, dinner at one, supper at nine, bed at eleven were parts of this routine; and, 'at half-past ten, let who would be there, he knocked out his last pipe'.

Other Breeders

Although Bakewell is the best known of the Leicestershire horse breeders, he was but one of many. William Pitt and, later, Trow-Smith, point this out. In *Rural Economy of the Midland Counties*, William Marshall writes: 'The district abounds, and has, for many years, abounded, with intelligent and spirited breeders. I could mention some fifteen or twenty men of repute, and most of them men of considerable property, who are in the same department [as Bakewell] and several of them eminent for their breeds of stock.'

Marshall describes how livestock men travelled a great deal, attending different markets, but he thought that in 1790 the spirit of improvement was at its peak. There were giants in the land in those days. . . .

Joan Grundy mentions a tombstone in the churchyard at Swithland, between Loughborough and Leicester, which carries a superb relief of three horses ploughing. The tomb is dated 1740 on the east side, 1745 on the west, and records the deaths of Sir Joseph and Dame Frances Danvers in 1743 and 1759 respectively. The reliefs indicate a good stamp of heavy horse, which Joan Grundy suggests may have been established in the district before 1750. If so, Bakewell had top-class material on which to start close at hand.

Robert Bakewell was a great stockbreeder but a poor communicator. For one thing, he disliked the few agricultural writers of the day, men who to us appear trustworthy. Some of his ideas about breeding were incestuous, and so opposed to religious teaching at the time – and yet he was a religious man.

He tells us nothing of the Fen Blacks, and his omission is the greater loss because no one else writes of them either. All we know is that around the time of Bakewell's death in 1795, there was a Fen type and a Midlands type of heavy horse. The Fen Black was not necessarily the jet black beloved by modern turn-out owners, but occurred in several gradations of the colour, starting at black-grey. It was a heavy, clumsy animal and it had masses of feather. The Lincolnshire soil allowed for full development.

Derbyshire heavies were also black, but their bone had more quality, from the limestone on which they grew. Further west in Staffordshire, brown was the prevailing colour. Bays, which by definition have black manes and tails, were then unknown in the heavy-horse world.

The Packington Blind Horse

This animal is chronicled as a founder of the Shire breed, but the line between mythology and fact is hard to trace. It is known that there was a 'Packington Blind (or "Blinded") Horse' which served mares in Leicestershire, Derbyshire and Warwickshire from about 1755 to 1770. He was said to stand on short legs and good feet and pasterns. Apparently he was black, with white face and markings. The blood of several of his numerous offspring was mingled in the horse William the Conqueror 2343. His height

10 William Marshall wrote of Bakewell's Shire stallion: 'A man of moderate size seemed to shrink behind his fore-end, which rose so perfectly upright that his ears stood (as Mr Bakewell says every horse's ears ought to stand!) perpendicularly over his fore feet.' It is not known whether this Boultbee engraving is of 'K' from life studies done earlier or of another Bakewell stallion. 'K' died about 1785

was about 16.2 hands, and he was described as being thick-set, with a low forehand.

How was it that a blind horse should be used for so long? Even in those days of ignorance on many hereditary matters, it seems unlikely that a horse that had lost his sight through disease would be used on mares to produce work horses that needed to see where they were going. The stud owners and grooms may not have understood genes, but they could observe their fellows and other stock.

'Bruni' in *Studies in Stock Breeding*, published in Melbourne, Australia, in 1902, states: 'Blindness in horses is so well known to be hereditary in some families that a stallion which is wholly or partially blind, unless injury to the eyes was caused by accident, is regarded as unsound and unfit for breeding purposes.'

Throughout the Napoleonic Wars, from 1795 to 1815 and the Peace of Amiens, there were no co-ordinated breeding attempts, nor any schemes to harness Britain's agricultural potential. After the war, things went from bad to worse in the heavy-horse world.

European frontiers were redrawn, and many countries were desperately short of good horses, heavies included. Dealers came to Britain, bid and bought. The country was almost denuded of sound breeding stock.

To intensify the troubles, the Board of Agriculture was dissolved in 1822. Farming was suffering a post-war depression which forced many farmers to sell anything which would realise good profits to remain in business. Hay and corn harvests were largely hand operations anyway, so tenants sold their best horses and made do with what was left.

In this depression there was neither the incentive nor the capital to invest in the future, so any horse that would sire a foal was used. Assorted local types had sprung up, but there was still nothing that could be called a Shire; Clydesdale historians have firmer ground on which to work in this period.

2 The Nineteenth Century

Queen Victoria's accession in 1837 coincided with better farming times. Ironically, heavy-horse breeding did not immediately respond. Cattle and sheep were paying well, could be bred in large numbers, and improvements were rapidly effected. Livestock breeds that made Britain the stud farm of the world were cradled in this period.

The advent of steam ploughing seemed to signal the end of the horse's supremacy. It did not. Nor did the railways. Rather they enhanced the need for horse power, to move the Industrial Revolution's goods to the station, away again to warehouses at the other end, and thence to retail shops and housewives' doors.

During all this time, some of the best English heavies were sold into Scotland, a process which was reversed after World War Two, thus effectively mixing the two races.

11 The heavy Black Horse was chiefly found in the Midland counties from Lincolnshire to Staffordshire, according to Youatt's 1840 edition of *The Horse*. This illustration is from the 1885 edition, but the text is the same. The engraving shows a dray-horse from a London stable. He was bred in Leicestershire, out of a Berkshire mare by a Wiltshire horse. His grand-sire was Flanders-bred and his granddam a Wiltshire mare.

How the draught horse incurred sprain of the back, cured by Elliman's Embrocation

Diseases

In the early nineteenth century there was scant knowledge of hereditary disease and unsoundness. Roaring, sidebones, ringbones, whistling, bone spavin, cataract, stringhalt or defective genital organs were eventually the subject of veterinary tests at the London Shows, starting in 1880, but up to then little was done. Until the middle of the century reading and writing were by no means common attributes among owners and grooms. The agricultural press, which today highlights every new development in the next issue, was then unknown in its present form.

Lawrence Drew

Noteworthy among those who bridged the gap between Bakewell's death in 1795 and the formation of the English Cart Horse Society in 1878, was Lawrence Drew of Merryton. He was factor or manager for the Duke of Hamilton, a name with extensive heavy-horse connections. Later he farmed on his own account, and blended Shire and Clyde successfully enough to encourage him to publish the *Select Clydesdale Stud Book*.

Drew's hope was for an amalgamation of the two British breeds. He bought and sold many Shires in the Midlands, and so keen was his judgment that he was known to pick out an exceptional animal from one glance through a railway carriage window, and stop at the next halt to retrace his footsteps in search of the animal he had spotted. On one occasion the farmer would not sell the best of his team by itself, so Drew bought the whole team which he had seen ploughing from his carriage window.

The most celebrated stallion bought in England by Drew was Lincolnshire Lad 1196, who died in his possession in 1878. This horse, foaled in 1866, was bred by William Whetton of Sutton Scarsdie, Chesterfield,

Derbyshire, in which locality he won several prizes before passing through three more hands and heading north. He was also known as 'K' and as Honest Tom 1196.

Lincolnshire Lad's son was the grey Lincolnshire Lad II 1365, grandsire of Rokeby Harold. We are now coming into recorded history, for the stallion Rokeby Harold was champion at the London Show as a yearling, a three-year-old and a four-year-old. As a two-year-old he was second to Bury Victor Chief.

Markeaton Royal Harold, the 1897 champion, was another grandson of Lincolnshire Lad. Among the females was Flora, by Drew's horse and bought by him in Derbyshire, who became dam of the great winner Pandora and of Prince of Clay. Prince of Clay, Handsome Prince and Pandora's Prince were all Clydesdale stallions and top-class breeders.

The Royal Agricultural Society of England

In 1838 The English Agricultural Society was founded. Two years later it was incorporated by Royal Charter as The Royal Agricultural Society of England, and has so remained to this day.

For almost 20 years before its formation, England had lacked a national body to invigorate farming. The old Board of Agriculture had died in 1822,

13 Cart mare and foal in that delightful *Series of the Mothers*, still available from Fores. This was painted by J.F. Herring Senior, and engraved by J. Harris in 1854. Like most Victorian animal painters, Herring really understood his subjects, and we may be sure that bone and feather are faithfully reproduced. The mare is not so heavy as her counterparts around the turn of the century, and would in fact be ideal for today's needs

14 Travelling cart stallion. Undated, but from early in Victoria's reign. The type is like the Clydesdale's forebears, but the pony does not look Scottish. Stallion grooms used to be provided with ponies, but tended to stay too long at the pub, and make up time with a smart trot! Stallion owners did not consider this conducive to fertility and the well-being of a horse covering many mares in a day

having languished since Waterloo. As the Government department which is now the Ministry of Agriculture was not formed until 1889, R.A.S.E. held the fort for half a century. It found plenty to do. Its official history records:

Of the three draught breeds of horses the Old English Black Horse [the Shire] was still rather variable in type, in keeping with the wide range of country which it occupied and the variety of land on which it was bred. The Clydesdale and the Suffolk were more uniform and more definite breeds. The Cleveland Bay had spread to some extent beyond its native district, and was in larger request for stage and private coaches.

The other noteworthy occurrence recorded by the Society was the first actual trial of steam power for tillage in 1836. But the shadows of that event took long in reaching the Shire.

The new agricultural society made energetic and rapid progress. It adopted Earl Spencer's suggestion for its motto: 'Practice with Science'. It pushed on to organize its first Country Meeting in July 1839 at Oxford.

The price of admission was one shilling, and 12,000 tickets were printed. When these ran out, committee members were deputed to take gate money, and the attendance topped 20,000. The huge crowd watched ten cart stallions compete for a £20 prize (it is little more today), and the winner was a Suffolk. Of the six cart mares entered, the winner is believed to have been a Shire. There was also a class for groups of five oxen, won by Herefords with Devons second.

The second show was staged at Cambridge in 1840. Classes in the cart horse section were provided only for stallions and for mares with foals, but at Liverpool in 1841 second prizes were added. The following season at Bristol saw extra classes for two-year-old colts and two-year-old fillies.

From the names and addresses of exhibitors, we may deduce that most of the animals on show belonged to strains later amalgamated in the Shire *Stud Book*, but several times famous Suffolk studs like Crisp's and Catlin's beat the Shires.

At Cambridge and Liverpool there were classes for pairs and single horses 'at plough', in connection with a ploughing match organized by the local committee.

From R.A.S.E.'s birth to the formation of the heavy-horse breed societies in the late 1870s, the original classification of heavy horses by type rather than breed was retained. Suffolks took most of the honours, and were lumped under 'Agricultural Horses' along with the various local strains that were later brought together in the Shire breed.

The years 1853–61 were prosperous for British agriculture. Steam engines and tile drainage commanded much interest, and on the draught-horse side, the best Shire types came from south Lincolnshire and Leicestershire, both fertile districts.

Teething troubles were experienced in the early years of The Shire Horse Society concerning registration with R.A.S.E. The name Shire was used from 1882. Should classes be limited to registered Shires, or should non-pedigree animals be eligible? R.A.S.E. had the encouragement of pedigree breeding as one of its aims, but the Shires were as yet diverse and their society insecure. In 1883 and 1884 special classes were arranged to cater for these non-pedigree animals, but R.A.S.E.'s dilemma was solved by low entries and poor quality. The Shire breed became soundly established, and classes for unregistered agricultural horses at later shows do not appear to have caused controversy.

15 Twenty of Young's Shire horses on parade at Young's Brewery in Wandsworth in 1967. They were marking the centenary of a beam engine 'erected for twenty horse power' in February 1867, and at work ever since at the brewery, providing power for pumping, milling and mashing

Half a century of R.A.S.E. shows was celebrated at Windsor in 1889, and the centenary was staged at the same place just before World War Two broke out. In 1889 Shires filled nine classes with 167 entries, and though the 1939 classes were increased to 12, entries dropped to 90. The shape of things to come was seen in the jumping entries, not provided for in 1889 but totalling 315 in five crowded classes at the centenary. Suffolk entries for the two shows were 105 and 168, Percherons nil and 109, and Clydesdales 93 and 50. The breeding classes for draught horses were generally good in 1939, with an outstanding display of four-horse teams in harness. Though Suffolks were most numerous, the first prize Shire team of four quite outstanding greys was favourite with many horsemen. Teams of six were also paraded.

Throughout its first century, and until the establishment of R.A.S.E.'s permanent showground in 1963 the event moved round annually. The colossal cost and organization involved increased yearly, and as the number of patrons able to offer their services free declined, the number of paid staff has increased, until we find the giant organization that R.A.S.E. has become today.

3 The Society

Early Steps

The mid-nineteenth century saw the founding of the early breed societies. They followed the *General Stud Book* for Thoroughbred horses, which was the world's first in 1808. Second came *Coates Herd Book*, for Shorthorn cattle, begun by an energetic man who rode a white horse around the northern breeders of reds, whites and roans, and whose concentrated labours were first brought to fruition in 1822.

Later in the century, other sheep and cattle breeds followed suit. There was no particular reason why the Shires should lag, but neither in those more easy-going times did there appear any need to hurry.

However, in March 1878 a meeting was held at the Farmers' Club, London, when a paper was read by Mr Frederick Street. It had been previously arranged that the formation of a heavy-horse society be

16 The Shire stallion England's Glory in 1825. He was 'allowed to be by the first judges the finest animal in the Kingdom in point of symetry and strength never equalled.' (*Walkers Quarterly*). There are 53 stallions named England's Glory in the first four volumes of the *Shire Horse Society Stud Book*! This one is listed first, and owned by Mr William Bingham, of Bingham Lodge, Holbeach, Lincolnshire. Foaled in 1814, he was brown, and out of a mare by Odham's Horse of Thorney Fen. His sire was Honest Tom 1060, foaled in 1800, at the dawn of recorded Shire history

proposed, and Frederick Street himself moved the resolution to form 'The English Cart Horse Society'. The seconder was Mr J.K. Fowler of Aylesbury, and the proposition was adopted unanimously, under the initial and temporary secretaryship of the proposer. In May a meeting of the Council was held under the chairmanship of the Earl of Ellesmere, again at the Farmers' Club. In June 1878 Mr G.M. Sexton became secretary.

'The retention of the word "English" would exclude Ireland, while the term "Cart Horse" is too general,' declared the Chairman, the Hon. E. Coke. 'The correct definition of their breed was that they were "Shires".' He described the horses at the Kilburn Park Royal Show, 1879 (then on London's western edge) as '"Dray Horses". They were big, heavy and strong horses, and it was clear from the judging yesterday that "the bigger they are, the heavier they are, and the more hair they have got the more likely they are to win prizes"'.

The Chairman then put the resolution: that the name of the Society be changed from The English Cart Horse Society of Great Britain and Ireland to The Shire Horse Society.

Mr Street's contrary amendment was rejected by 49 votes to 36. The original resolution was submitted and adopted by 52 votes to 33. Mr Thomas Brown thereupon demanded a poll. At their next meeting the Council decided to take legal advice, a practice to which it has been prone ever since.

The question of naming remained in abeyance until February 1883, when it was resurrected without result. But a year later the alteration was carried

17 Harold. 'We have seen finer horses than Harold 3703, but we have yet to find a sire equal to him as a getter of grand equine stock'. This verdict in *Livestock in Health and Disease, c.* 1900, has stood the test of time, for all modern strains may be traced back to Harold. By the Grey Lincolnshire Lad II, he was foaled in 1881, and lived till 1901

by an overwhelming majority, and the official name became: The Shire Horse Society of the United Kingdom of Great Britain and Ireland.

Membership

Membership was 376 in 1880, and 903 when the name was changed in 1884. The next year it rose to four figures, climbing past the 2,000 mark in 1895, and to 3,029 in 1901. By 1911 it had reached 4,000, and the 5,000 milestone was passed after World War One, to reach a peak of 6,491 just before the slump really took effect in 1922.

British breed societies have been singularly fortunate in the calibre and loyalty of their officials. In its first 104 years the Shire Horse Society has had only five secretaries.

Mr G.M. Sexton served as auctioneer and secretary until 1883, continuing as auctioneer for a further 11 years. Daily precision and supervision were demanded of the secretary of a growing and flourishing society, and the man to fit the bill proved to be John Sloughgrove. He was persuaded to leave the assistant secretaryship of the Royal Agricultural Society, and his reluctance was so well overcome that he stayed for 33 years. Under his rule the Society became dubbed 'The Sloughgrove Horse Society'!

High Prices

In the 1880s, things were really warming up in the newly-born Shire world. Wealthy patrons vied with each other to secure the best, and Shire breeding ranked almost as high in the interests of the landed gentry as land owning itself.

Sir Walter Gilbey paid a high price for the Buckinghamshire-bred Spark to R.W. Rowland, which was followed by Lord Wantage's successful bid of £1,500 or guineas for Prince William, owned by John Rowell.

J. Albert Frost tells us that the next sensational private sale was that of Bury Victor Chief, for 2,500 guineas from the same vendor. The horse was Royal Show champion in 1891, and the buyer Joseph Wainwright.

Also in 1891, 18 of Premier's offspring were paraded with their sire at A.C. Duncombe's Calwich sale. Despite the number of foals among them, they averaged £273. Chancellor 4959 at six years old topped the line up at 1,100 guineas. A tree was planted at the spot where Chancellor stood while the four-figure bid for him mounted, and the next year Premier was buried at one side of it. Harold was buried on the other side in 1901, and the ground was surrounded by railings and lovingly preserved.

More Records

Another kind of record was set up in 1892, when a stallion was hired for £1,000 to serve 100 mares. The horse was Vulcan 4145, owned by the Earl of Ellesmere, and bred by John Whitehead at Medlar Hall, Kirkham, Lancashire, whose descendants are enthusiastic Shire supporters today.

Vulcan was London Show champion in 1891, and proof that these top stallions were no mere flashes in the pan comes from Albert Frost: 'Since then a thousand pounds for a first class sire has been paid many times, and it is in districts where they have been used that those in search of the best go for their foals.'

The fortunate, or far seeing, hirers of Vulcan were the shrewd tenant farmers who formed the Welshpool Shire Horse Society, and it is worthy of note that the male and female champions of the 1914 London Show were both bred in the Welshpool district – Champion's Goalkeeper and Lorna Doone.

Other four-figure bids of the 1890s were for Arkwright's Marmion to Fred Crisp, for 1,400 guineas in 1892; Waresley Premier Duke to Victor Cavendish, later Duke of Devonshire, for 1,000 guineas at W.H.O. Duncombe's 1897 sale; and the same figure by the same buyer for Lord Llangattock's Hendre Crown Prince that same year.

4 The Turn of the Century

Edwardian Days

The years before 1914. . . . So many who lived then regarded them as a peak, since when nothing has been the same, or anywhere near as good. To those of us who missed that era, the recollections of a former generation lend it a golden glow. For the best things in life, cricket and Shire horses included, it was indeed the Golden Age.

We cannot assess the Shire's place in isolation. The social and monetary state of those concerned with it colour the picture, and agriculture most of all. Farm men were existing on £1 a week and working long hours, often six till six in the fields and with no Saturday afternoon holiday.

The working man's status was too often disregarded. Grooms were highly skilled, plentiful – and cheap. Tenant farmers operated under a more feudal system than today. They could be put off their farm for not attending church, or for bagging a pheasant, and if they presumed to use a stallion other than that provided by the estate, they could not look on the next rent day with equanimity.

Yet for all its injustices, ostentation and social inequalities, the period

19 Bury Victor Chief was a black with three white legs, foaled in 1889. One of the truly enduring names in Shire history, his five years of top show success followed wins for his offspring. He was sold as a two-year-old for 2,500 guineas

20 Buscot Harold. Like his sire, Markeaton Royal Harold, Buscot Harold was hired by the Welshpool Society. His stint was in 1901, after which he travelled in Peterborough, Lincolnshire and west Staffordshire. He was first and champion at the Birmingham Royal of 1898, and again at Maidstone the year following. He was foaled in 1896

1900–14 had so much to offer. It held out hope. People really did believe that they would be better off next year.

Enterprising farm workers could become their own bosses, starting with a small place on a big estate. The squire often provided a quality stallion for his tenants, and spare teams in case of sickness.

For the Shire breeder, the turn of the century was a period of undoubted improvement. Demand for quality horses in the towns had never been so high. So instead of a tractor depreciating at several hundred or even thousand pounds a year, the farmer's power units appreciated.

This was not all fun. A former East Riding horseman told me how he would patiently bring out a team of young five- or six-year-old Shires, have them working nicely and quietly, and along would come the boss with the dreaded words: 'Loose those two out and give them a show along the headland!' The potential buyer accompanying him would inspect from behind and fore, and if a deal was struck he might depart with his purchases there and then. No stable goodbyes. Not even a chance for a final grooming. Just an empty plough and the prospect of tackling a pair of raw youngsters in the morning. The horseman's acquired arts would be used to quieten them and bring them to the same state of perfection – ready for the next buyer.

Details of work on the land are given elsewhere (see Chapter 9). The horsemen carrying it out were deeply interested in the top show horses, and even more so in the travelling stallions derived from them. It is fitting to start with Lockinge Forest King, as he was responsible for setting the stamp of Shire favoured at that time, both for good and ill.

The Craze for Feather – Lockinge Forest King

Lockinge Forest King 18867 was a bay, foaled in 1899 and bred by Lady
Wantage at Lockinge, Wantage. His sire was Lockinge Manners 16780, and
his dam The Forest Queen 4470, by Royal Albert 1885.

Forest King was sold to J.P. Cross, Catthorpe Towers, Rugby, and later
to W.T. Everard, of Bardon Hall, Leicester. He was assessed by Gilbert H.
Parsons in 1907 as 'possibly the most successful sire the breed has yet seen.
He is sire of the Champion Foal at Ashbourne three years in succession, Five
First Prize Winners and both Champions at the R.A.S. of E., Lincoln,
1907'.

The Forest Queen was also dam of other good horses – Lockinge Albert,
Royal William II and Lockinge Forester. Her most famous son Forest King
was the spark that set off the craze for feather. If a young horse had plenty of
feather, it was already half sold. It might be lacking in middle and have a
head like a turnip, and moderate limbs, but if they were clothed with plenty
of feather the horse's other qualities seemed to matter little.

Farmers and breeders, then as now, were concerned with cash above most
things. They may have been Shire fanatics, intent on breeding the perfect
animal for the joy of it, but to do so a high ranking stallion was needed, and
perhaps a nicely bred filly to augment the home stud. Such items needed
cash, and if a hairy-legged foal sold for more than a cleaner-limbed
youngster, the hairy one would be the aim. The British stockbreeder can
breed anything under the sun if there's money in it.

Albert Clark, who made most judging appearances at the London Show,

33

22 An interesting study of Tatton Friar aged four (*top*) and then aged seven. Never slight, he filled out into a magnificent horse, and sired excellent stock. His two-year-old son Friar John made 600 guineas at the Shire Horse Show auction in 1907

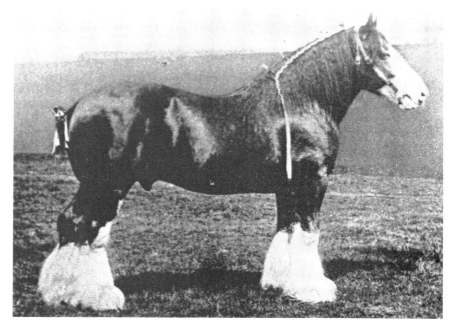

said: 'This feather was a great help to some of our grooms who are artists, and who can make a bad-shaped leg like a good one.' Tom Forshaw added: 'Give me some hair, and I can make a leg.'

Just as some of our show sheep would look mighty peculiar if they were clipped first, so those hairy Shires would appear very different if they were walked through a pond.

Lockinge Forest King stood at 20 guineas a mare, or approaching 20 times a groom's weekly wage. Though not many tenant farmers could afford such

a fee, and indeed were usually too far distant from the stallion, they could and did use the hairy horse's sons.

If home sales were helped by feather, exports were not. The prairies and arable land in the New World grew corn after corn, and consequently weed after weed (there were no weed sprays in those days). Some particularly obnoxious weeds had burr seeds, which stuck to the horse's fetlocks in their thousands if the hair offered any sort of grip. Forest King's descendants were for this reason unpopular across the sea; the cleaner-legged Clydesdale and the feather-free Percheron were more to the taste of the big-team drivers, whose horses ambled in front of the hitch cart ten, 20 or 30 strong. There was no grooming as we know it, no finesse; a couple of good lead horses sufficed, with the rest packed in behind.

The big-team drivers had very definite opinions about brushing out the burrs from 80 or 120 hairy legs at the end of a day, so Lockinge Forest King and his ilk did not rate amongst their favourite stallions. And as all implements there had seats, a fast-walking animal was essential. The best teams walked 20 miles in a ten-hour day. Anything giving the impression of sluggishness was not wanted. The immaculate care given by the British horseman to his pair, morning and night, was out of the question.

The owner of Lockinge Forest King, in less exacting home conditions, did not need to worry over-much about the prairie horses. Had not a whole string of top prize winners been born to the Royal Agricultural Society of England Champion?

23 Where all the hair came from. Lockinge Forest King in July 1907. Look at the colossal amount of feather on those snowy hind pasterns, and consider grooming such a horse after a day's ploughing on heavy land. Equally relevant, imagine a skilled groom setting out the hair to disguise a poor leg

Extended pedigree of Lockinge Forest King 18867

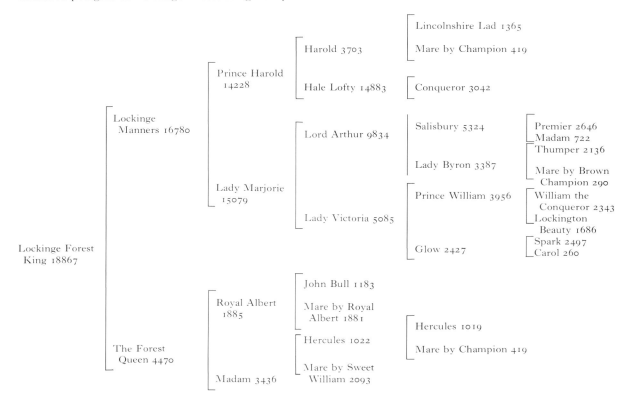

Other Sires

Forest King's son, King Forest 24347 was a brown, foaled in 1905, and standing 16.3 hands high. Out of Lockinge Dimple, he was bred by H.R. Craig, Billesdon, Leicester, and owned by F.E. Muntz, Umberslade, Hockley Heath, Birmingham. He won the Open and Foal Ashbourne Cup in 1905, and was first at the Royal the following year, while in 1907 his first prizes again included the Royal at Lincoln, the Welsh National and the Bath and West.

Lockinge Forest King's daughters to win at the Lincoln Royal, 1907, were Ashleigh Royal Duchess 50089, and Bardon Flower of the Forest (Vol. 29). The former was a bay with four white feet, foaled in 1905, and bred by Gamble Bros. of Braunstone, Leicester, before making a short move to Bardon Hall and W.T. Everard. Her next owner was W. Whitley and her price 460 guineas. Bardon Flower of the Forest was sold at the Bardon Hall sale of 1907 to F.E. Muntz for 230 guineas. She also gained firsts that year at Nottinghamshire, Derbyshire, Staffordshire, Royal Lancashire, Leicester-shire and Moreton-in-Marsh shows – notable Shire strongholds then and now.

Ratcliffe Conquering King 24548 was a Lockinge Forest King colt, foaled in 1905, who would be in tremendous demand today, if his massive girth, his bay colouring with its one white foot among the black, could be reincarnated among modern Shires. He stood reserve to his half-brother King Forest at the 1905 Ashbourne (Derbyshire) show as a foal, and was bred and owned by Frank Farnsworth of Tooley Park, Hinckley, Leicestershire.

This owner evidently had a liking for Lockinge Forest King, for the 1908 *Stud Book* lists four of his colts at Tooley Park. They are Ratcliffe Charming King, bought from J.L. Harrison, Pailton Fields, Rugby, and three home-bred ones, Ratcliffe Coming King, Ratcliffe Draughtsman and Ratcliffe King Albert.

All were bay or brown with very little white. Charming King had a white off-hind foot, Coming King white hind heels, Draughtsman black legs and King Albert white hind fetlocks.

Others in the lengthy list of prizewinners sired by Lockinge Forest King are Lawford Diamond 48506, Ratcliffe Forest King 23622, Redlynch Forest King 23626, and a sweet mare, Bardon Marion. She was champion at the Royal in 1907, and successful at a string of major events in that year.

24 A page of foals. They have reached these tremendous sizes in under five months. The bay colt out of Dunsmore Combine (bottom left) was not foaled until 25 April, and was photographed in July

COLT FOAL.—*Sire Redlynch Forest King, Dam Dorothy of Warcies.*
(August, 1907.)

FILLY FOAL.—*Sire Starling Jameson, Dam Starling Harold's, Last.*
(August, 1907.)

COLT FOAL.—*Sire Forest King, Dam Dunsmore Combine.*

COLT FOAL.—*Sire Dunsmore Jameson, Dam Tatton Iris.*

HOWARD & JONES, PRINTERS.

37

25 Lockinge Truffle 23453 – just the stamp of horse to be a pin-up in a working horse stable of King Edward VII's reign. Sadly, photographs were rare then, and mostly beyond the reach of single horsemen living in on farms. Truffle was black, foaled in 1904 and by Lockinge Forester, own brother to Lockinge Forest King. He was reserve champion at the Lincoln Royal in 1907

Noble Influence

The extent to which the upper classes of the time dominated the Shire show world is indicated in the magnificent, dark-green hard-backed R.A.S.E. *Catalogue* for 1902. The Royal Show that year was at Carlisle, and to the 182 well laid-out pages of entries were added 30 of advertisements. The cloth cover continues to form a pencil holder.

The class for Shire stallions foaled in 1900 contained ten entries, of whom six owners were titled people, two of them MPs. Of five owners entering for Shire mare with foal at foot, only Philo L. Mills of Ruddington Hall, Nottinghamshire, was neither an MP nor an earl, and his brown mare Saxon Girl was bred by Sir Walter Gilbey.

Shire fillies foaled in 1900 had among their owners an earl, a lord, four baronets and an MP. Of the four other mortals, William Jackson of The Hall, Knottingley, Yorkshire, had bought his chestnut filly Hendre Bessie from Lord Llangattock, who showed Hendre Birthright by Prince Harold. And above all there was the intense royal interest of King Edward VII.

Clydesdales

It is interesting that at that Carlisle Royal, staged only a few miles from the Scottish border, Clydesdale entries totalled 84, against 63 Shires and 18 Suffolks. Farmers came into their own in the agricultural classes for geldings, mares and fillies. Many of these were of Clydesdale extraction, as would be expected as Cumberland, Northumberland and Durham were strongholds of the Scottish breed.

The most remarkable aspect of the show was that of those 84 entries, no fewer than 25 were sired by the famous Baron's Pride. Any Shire enthusiast would surely travel 200 miles tomorrow to see that horse. He would add to the stature of either breed. Foaled in 1890, before Shire and Clydesdale had really separated, he was champion at the Royal Highland on his only appearance in 1894, and had the foundation sire Darnley twice among his great-grandparents. Of his hundreds of prize winning offspring, his grandson Dunure Footprint was the most famous.

Baron's Pride dominated the list of winning sires in 1896, and at the 1899

26 The black Hendre Champion was foaled in 1898. He was by Prince Harold out of Jemson's Belle, a Garstang, Lancashire-bred mare, from a line of successful Shires. Though Hendre Champion had his share of prizes, including second at the London Shire Horse Show of 1901, he was best known for his offspring. At the Norbury Park sale in 1907, seven of his two-year-old fillies averaged £139. 4s., among them Norbury Juno, who topped the sale at 400 guineas

27 Blythwood Guelder Rose was one of the great Shire females. Foaled in 1895, she was by Prince Harold and out of a Hitchin Conqueror mare, Tudor Rose. She was a brown, and embarked as a yearling on a winning career that spanned a decade. In fact she won bigger events as she got older, being first and reserve champion at the 1903 London Shire Horse Show, first and champion at the 1904 Royal Show, first again at the Shire Horse Show of 1905, and first and reserve champion at the Derby Royal in 1906. She had three excellent offspring, one of them born across the Atlantic, where she died

Royal Highland his offspring claimed over half the prizes. He regained the winning title in 1908 when he was 18, so it is no surprise to see his outstanding progeny vying for the farmers' favour against the Shires at the Carlisle Royal.

Wallace, in *Farming Livestock of Great Britain*, 1903, had no doubts about the similarities between the Shire and the Clydesdale and of the benefits of inter-breeding: 'The points of the best specimens are very much like those of the Clydesdale horse. The ordinary varieties of the two breeds differ more in appearance than the better sorts, which, as has been explained, are probably more closely related than farmers generally suppose.'

5 The Great War and After

Wounded horses. . . . It's unendurable. It is the moaning of the world, it is the martyred creation, wild with anguish, filled with terror, and groaning.

E.M. Remarque, *All Quiet on the Western Front.*

In the Great War of 1914–18, half a million horses died or were put down in British Army service alone. By August 1915, Army horse numbers had risen from the peacetime strength of 25,000 to 535,000. Despite continual casualties, the number reached 870,000 two years later.

It is invidious to compare the sufferings of one breed against others in such carnage, and we can but surmise the numbers of Shires and Shire-types. Heavy draughts constituted about one-fifth of British Army horse strength at the War's end, and despite the many Percherons, Shires were used in their thousands.

During the War, the shortage of skilled horsemen at home made itself felt most heavily on the pedigree Shire studs. There was a call to release stallion men from the services for the April/June period, but as the war progressed this became more difficult to achieve without depleting units in the field. Their cream had already gone. Men competent to foal a mare were also scarce, although when presented with the situation, the older ones at home

28 Horses going to war. The Shires suffered along with the rest of the human and equine world in 1914–18

All accounts not paid by 10th July, 10 - will be charged for collecting.

All Mares tried by any of the Highfield Horses and afterwards put to others, or sold, or exchanged will be charged the full fee.

Mares are only taken at owners risk.

No Mare will be served twice under 11 days.

Excellent accommodation for Mares at grass— Mare and Foal, 8 6 ; Barren Mares, 7 - per week.

No business on Sundays.

Station—Leek.

Telegrams "Nicholson, Leek."

Entrance to Stud Farm, Abbey Green Road.

GROOM,

E. WILLIAMS.

For further particulars apply to

Mr. R. L. FALKNER,
ESTATE OFFICE,
HIGHFIELD, LEEK.

"Dunsmore Royal Friar."
(29337.)

PHOTO BY G. H. PARSONS

SEASON 1917.

THE PROPERTY OF

SIR ARTHUR NICHOLSON,
HIGHFIELD HALL,
LEEK, Staffs.

---

29 Stud cards have a fascination that grows with the years

were able to cope and the farm women played their full part.

In the four months following the Armistice on 11 November 1918, a quarter of a million horses were repatriated, and disposed of at an average of about £30 each.

The Society During the War

In the first November of the War, Sir Walter Gilbey died, aged 83. He had been President of R.A.S.E. and the Hackney and Hunter breed societies as well as the Shire's. He left, among other things, a legacy of livestock books handsomely bound in gilt, and the Cart Horse Parade.

Another notable death was Baron Rothschild's, in 1915. A highly successful exhibitor, his stud was dispersed at record prices. The 32 males and 15 females averaged over £564 with half of them youngsters.

Deservedly, Baron Rothschild's manager Tom Fowler took over as tenant, retaining Birdsall Menestral, twice London champion and four times reserve (fig. 21).

In the following year, John Sloughgrove died. He had been Society secretary since 1883 (see page 29). The war ended with the Society intact and an all-time high of *Stud Book* entries – 911 stallions and 5,483 mares.

Meanwhile another threat from across the Channel was emerging. Percheron imports infuriated the jingoistic Shire breeders of the time, and were linked with motor cars as 'the common enemy'. One benefit of the

"DUNSMORE ROYAL FRIAR."

23337

BROWN, Foaled 1908.

SIRE, Tatton Friar 21953.
G. „ Conquering Harold 15558.
DAM, 48934 Oadby Bonny by Brandon Royalty 18563.
G. „ 25248 Ashwell Lads Love by Merry Lad 2626.
G.G. „ 19213 Ashwell Flower by Reality 2882.
WILL TRAVEL THIS SEASON.

PRIZES WON.

1914.—H.C. S.H.S. London.

DUNSMORE ROYAL FRIAR is an exceedingly good getter.

PRIZES WON BY HIS STOCK:

1913,—First Staff. County. Wolverhampton.
„ First and Two Cups, value 50gs. Tutbury.
„ Second, Bakewell. Second, Uttoxeter.
1914.—Second, Meynell Hunt. Second, Leek.
„ First and 20gs. Cup, Bakewell.
„ First. Alstonefield.
„ First (£10) and Reserve for Champion, Crewe.
At last year's S.H.S., London, 3 animals by him all in the money.
Foals made up to 87 guineas last October Sales at Crewe.
Yearlings have been sold at £100 and £105. 2-year olds 105 and 125 gs.
DUNSMORE ROYAL FRIAR was H.C. at the London Show
last year, and holds a certificate of soundness from the Shire
Horse Show Veterinary Surgeons.

FEE £5 5s. 0d

TENANT FARMERS £3 3s. 0d.

Half fee to be paid at time of service, remainder
in February, 1918 if in foal.

GROOM'S FEE 2/6.

CERTIFICATE OF SOUNDNESS.

9th March, 1917—This is to certify I have this day examined by the
request of SIR ARTHUR NICHOLSON, a Brown Shire Stallion, "DUNSMORE
ROYAL FRIAR," 29337. I find the said animal to be 8 years old, and
sound. Signed GEORGE BOULTON, M.R.C.V.S.

ROUTE

(IF HEALTH PERMITS)

Monday—Leaves home at **10 a.m.** through Basford, to Mr. Heaths, Booths Hall Ipstones, for the night.

Tuesday—Leaves Booths Hall **10 a.m.** through Ipstones, Windy Harbour to Mr. E. Cottons Hurst Farm, Cauldon till Thursday morning.

Thursday—Leaves Hurst Farm, at **9 a.m.** through Waterfall, to the Shoulder of Mutton Inn at Grindon, (to Bait 1 hour,) then to Mr. Charles Stubbs, Yew Tree Farm, Wetton, for the night.

Friday—Leaves Yew Tree Farm, **10 a.m.** through Hulme End, to the Greyhound Hotel, Warslow, for the night.

Saturday—Leaves the Greyhound Hotel, at **10 a.m.** through Onecote, to Green Man, Bottomhouse, (to Bait 1 hour,) then through Bradnop for Home.

---

backs-to-the-wall fight to keep the heavy horse alive during the 1960s and '70s is the accord that exists among the three English breeds, Shire, Suffolk and British Percheron, even though horsey speakers from outside the heavy ranks have been known to make cheap inter-breed jibes.

The new secretary of the Shire Horse Society, A.B. Charlton, regarded the early 1920s Percheron incursion as 'an unmerited slur on our native horses at a time when all the world is expected to flock here to buy our incomparable livestock'.

There were grumblings that the Shire had been unsuitable for the strains of modern war. He got greasy legs if he stood without a dry bed; he could not thrive on poor or irregular rations; he did not like draughts. Of course not. War conditions would have tested the hardiest hill pony, used to a sparse diet but with nothing like that weight so essential to shift loads which breeders had bestowed on the 1920s' Shire.

For the heavy draught work for which he was bred, the Shire came through the War commendably. In any event, 1919 saw the enrolment of 700 new Society members, some of whom probably joined because of attacks on their native breed.

Their confidence was further boosted by a tremendous sale of Shire females at the Pendley stud. This had been sold by J.G. Williams to John Measures and his former manager, Harry Bishop, who staged a home sale. Half of the 34 females offered were foals or yearlings, yet the average was £733. 10s., a record.

30 Information on the horse and his route was contained in all stud cards

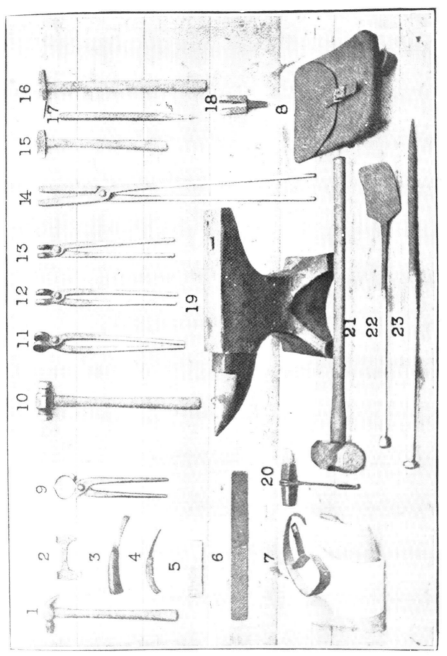

1. The Shoeing Hammer.
2. The Buffer.
3. The Drawing Knife.
4. The Searcher.
5. The Rasp.
6. The Ragstone.
7. The Apron.
8. The Farrier's Tool Bag.
9. The Pincers.

10. The Turning Hammer.
11. }
12. } Shoe Tongs.
13. }
14. Fire Tongs } Carried in the Tool Bag by the Farrier.
15. The Fuller.
16. The Stamp,
17. Pritchel, carried in the Tool Bag by the Farrier

18. The Heel Cutter, half-round.
19. Anvil.
20. The Set.
21. Sledge Hammer.
22. Shoe.
23. Poker.

After the War

Those who had survived the War wanted to live, and live extravagantly. They did. Forshaw's March King was hired to the Crewe Shire Horse Society for 1,000 guineas, or more than 500 times a working man's weekly wage. Then Theale Lockinge King went to the Montgomeryshire Society, home of many good Shires, for 1,500 guineas, and was engaged by the Crewe Society for the next year, to follow March King, at 2,000 guineas. Newark Shire Horse Society paid the same figure for March King for 1921. The fees have not been topped, in real or any other terms.

In Volume 42 of the *Stud Book*, issued in 1921, the 7,620 entries comprised 1,010 stallions and 6,599 mares. Never have such halcyon days been regained. But the slump was on hand.

That early-1920s slump has haunted those who lived through it ever since. It was sparked off by the repeal of the Corn Production Acts under which, not for the first time, a British Government withdrew all firm commitments to farming and turned it and the land adrift.

Those who had bought stock or farm the year before saw values tumble so swiftly that many were ruined. On the Yorkshire Wolds, farmers passed stock round from one to another to present a more solid outlook when unwanted creditors called. Landlord, tenant, and estate agent all tried to prop up one another. Land fell derelict and farms vacant in a quite unparalleled and unnecessarily abysmal period in British rural life, until World War Two caused a rethink.

Under the 1914–18 plough-up campaign, breeders of heavy horses had been officially encouraged to provide more motive power to till those extra two million acres – to breed from everything possible. Foals conceived and born in the midst of war came into work in 1921 and 1922. In addition, the demobilization of horses was as haphazard as that of the unfortunate soldiers, pushed onto a labour market with nothing to offer.

The Shire, for decades the best rent payer on the mixed farm, was more numerous than ever, and less in demand. The internal combustion engine and general unemployment caused a shortage of buyers for Shires, and those who would buy had little money.

One of the men under whom I learnt farming, Harry Rockliff, spoke often of those days in the Vale of York: 'We sold potatoes for five shillings a ton, which did not pay the cost of riddling them, but we had to have the money from somewhere. We stayed on the farm for weeks together. We dare not leave it, for fear of spending money we hadn't got.'

A lover of the working horse, he kept his Shire teams together, but gone was the remunerative market for the five-year-old, quiet in all gears and suited to city work. All breeders suffered, from the big pedigree stud owners to the working farmers.

Another of Harry Rockliff's stories touches the heartstrings. Half a dozen unbroken two- and three-year-olds were out watering in the confined farm yard. They would rear, kick and stamp and prance in their high spirits, then gallop in concert through the open gate. One day a small girl, a toddler, escaped from her mother's vigilance and crawled across the gateway. The young horses set off in their usual style, flat out for the gate with a pounding of great hooves, when from their midst an old Shire mare thrust herself to the fore. She jumped right over the little girl and parted the tearaways on either side.

Suffice it to say that that mare was never sold. She had 13 foals in 14 years,

31 Tools of the trade – the blacksmith's craft. The turning hammer (10) is interesting. It weighs about four pounds, has one flat and one convex face, and the sides are angular for the purpose of drawing clips. With one striker to help him, the smith uses this hammer in welding, but with two strikers he merely beats time on the anvil, and by the strength of his beat indicates the force he requires them to put into each blow. (From *Animal Management*, 1933)

and an intelligence comparable to Mr Frome's mare, described in the early Clydesdale *Stud Book* as being 'as wise as a man'.

From 1926 to 1931 there were tentative moves to unite Clydesdale and Shire officially, as they had indeed been united genetically decades before. But if the horses would mix, the men wouldn't, and rivalries deepened. Sadly, the more closely linked two livestock breeds are, the greater the rivalry and indeed jealousy between their respective owners seem to be.

In order to end the arguments about comparative merits, the Shire people organized a pulling demonstration in 1924. Two of the big geldings that worked in Liverpool's dockland were hitched to a $2\frac{1}{2}$-ton lorry with no springs, measuring $18\frac{1}{2}$ feet long and $7\frac{1}{2}$ feet wide. The geldings were shod in Liverpool fashion, with caulkins and toe pieces against the slippery granite setts, and walked away with a load of $18\frac{1}{2}$ tons.

The next test was made indoors. Two Shires moved a 6-ton load easily. They then pulled in a narrow corridor on worn wooden blocks, but there was no space for them to pull first to one side and then the other as they would normally do. Nevertheless they pulled $16\frac{1}{2}$ tons.

At the Wembley Exhibition, a pair of Shires was tested by a dynamometer. One horse pulled the equivalent of 12 tons when shod in flat shoes, but 29 tons in Liverpool shoes, a striking testimony to their worth apart from other considerations. Then the two, shod in Liverpool fashion, hauled the equivalent of a starting load of 50 tons. The Society let the world know of these achievements at the time and has continued to do so ever since!

Another justifiable claim of Shire fame arose through a move to ban the docking of horses' tails. A private member's bill, initiated by Colonel Burns, had already passed its second reading before the horse world or the Ministry of Agriculture knew anything about it. Shire Horse Society secretary A.B. Charlton immediately turned to his new President, Sir Walter Gilbey, who was well connected in high places and managed to persuade the existing powers to speak so strongly that the bill was withdrawn.

Not until 1929 did the surfeit of working horses right itself. Fewer had been bred, the Army dispersals had ceased their effects, and there was once again a market for geldings. Travelling stallions licensed by the Government showed a slight rise for the first time since 1921. At 716 they were below one-third of the 1920 total, but in general a steady climb occurred, reaching 1,075 in 1937.

6 The Shire's Demise

There were many valid reasons for encouraging more tractors in Britain during 1939–45, and fewer horses. An extra two million acres of ground were to be ploughed up, as a result of shameless Government neglect of agriculture between the wars. It was easier, and quicker, to teach a 'Land Girl' to drive a Fordson than a team.

The greatest real turning point in the use of literal horse power came *after* World War Two. It was a mental as well as a physical change. Young men, impatient as ever with the old ways, linked former depression with the heavy-horse era. They would have none of it. They intended to keep British farming on the high plane where it had been placed by German submarines, and never to allow it to be summarily discarded as happened in 1922.

In those early post-World War Two years, the machines almost swept the board. The machinery itself was cheap – by today's standards, very cheap – fuel was apparently inexhaustible, and very low in price. Speed was of the essence, and speed was then linked to the internal combustion engine.

Harry Ferguson, who was afraid of horses, and disliked them intensely, preached that the tractor could alleviate world poverty and hunger. Horses, he said, consumed much of the food they produced. On a ten-acre farm, horses used four acres for themselves. With them, the farmer had to work 1,000 hours to achieve the same results that a tractor could manage in 200.

Even allowing for considerable exaggeration, such statistics appeared unassailable. They encouraged the spirit of the times – more freedom, more leisure in a world of plenty freed from the blackout, ration books and restrictions.

This spirit was caught by farmers' sons and farm men. Progress and mechanization became synonymous. Those who bought the latest tractors, now being advertised in profusion after wartime curtailments, were 'with it'. Those who stuck to horses also stuck to their old cars, their old clothes, their old lifestyle. They did not fit into the late '40s and '50s.

In 1952 I started farming with a brand new Ferguson tractor, a two-furrow plough and transport box, total cost £420. This was for a 136-acre dales farm on a hillside. It was possible to get from one end to the other by driving flat out – the usual pace – in less time than a pair of horses could have been fetched from the field, harnessed and yoked.

At that time there was still an abundance of keen and capable young men on the land, brought up to work. And I had one of the best. If, as a relative suggested, I returned to a team of horses for cheapness, that man would have left the same week, laughed to scorn by his mates for 'going back to horses'.

Few, very few, horses were actually coming onto the land and being broken to harness. Those that still worked did so because they always had. By this time they were aged, quiet and reliable, knowing every inch of the

32 There are three Shires in this team, while a spade-lugged tractor in the background hauls another self-binder. (*International Harvester*)

33 Types of English farm waggons. They were made chiefly in the arable districts, where heavy horses were bred. Two-wheeled carts were more common in hilly districts and in Scotland. *From top to bottom*: A Hereford Waggon; Kent waggon; Gloucestershire 'hoop-raved' waggon

farm and able to take out fodder for cattle and sheep in winter and be guided, quite safely, by voice alone. They were part of the family. But when their natural day ended, they were almost never replaced.

The day of the Shire on the land was curtailed the more speedily through the very dedication and skill of some of its horsemen. Brought up in an age when the art of cultivation was all, they would never accept a lower standard. When they were young, in the '20s and before, crops could not be encouraged by fertilizers or safeguarded by weed sprays. There were none, on any scale. Good crops depended on proper ploughing, both for germination and burying 'rubbish', while the numerous weeds that appeared could only be dealt with in the root crops, by horse hoe followed by hand hoe.

Today's accepted rules of cost efficiency would have been despised then. If a man could plough an acre a day with two Shires and a single furrow and achieve perfection, he would not be prepared to use a two-furrow plough and three horses if the quality of the work was ever so slightly lower. He would be derided from the first pint until closing time.

A seat was anathema to that generation of horsemen. 'Encouraging

48

34 A ploughing day at Headley Hall Farm, Marley Hill, Northumberland, in 1937. Ploughing days or 'boon days' were given to incoming farmers taking over a new farm. The date of entry was commonly Lady Day, 25 March, or 5 April, which left insufficient time for the new man to 'get ploughed up' before seed time. Such events were semi-social occasions and minor ploughing matches, each ploughman trying to outdo the others. (*Beamish North of England Open Air Museum*)

idleness,' they termed it. Note that this attitude sprung from the employed men, not the farmers, although one North Riding farmer did say that he would never pay a man to 'sit on his backside' all day. Therefore when the first tractor arrived he drove it himself!

On one occasion I was rolling down some heavy clay, with brick-size clods, behind a pair of Shires. Even the Cambridge roller skated over the top of these clods, so I tentatively suggested fitting the seat from the grass mower, and riding, to add a little extra weight. The response of the boss (my uncle) was: 'Fill some bags with soil, and put them on. You'll expect to be paid for doing nowt [nothing] next.'

The routine of grooming and regular stable times became a cult. The time spent 'doing up' the horses simply did not pay as wages rose. When concerned with the management of a large farm near Scarborough, I was detailed to remind the one horseman that he should be on the land as quickly as were the tractor drivers. 'You know what he's been doing for the past quarter of an hour?' said the boss, 'He's been grooming that horse!'.

Chivers gives 1947 as the year of the great slaughter of heavies. George Ewart Evans regards 1952 as more applicable to the eastern counties, and that is probably true of northern England. At any rate, horses still predominated in the corn harvest of 1949.

One of the first jobs to be tractor-powered was cutting corn with a binder, and no horse lover can regret the change. The drive to reciprocate the knife and turn the canvases which elevated the cut corn came from the ground wheel or 'bull' wheel. In a wet spell this skidded constantly, and the team had to back the clumsy machine through their collars, joined to the pole by leather straps. Collars were designed for a forward pull, and pulled askew on their necks when backing was attempted. Added to this were the heat and the flies, for corn can be cut only after the dew has risen. Otherwise the canvases become wet and torn. On a large farm, with a change of horses, it was bearable. My grandfather in the East Riding drove four Shires in his binder, and changed two every hour. The saddler at Sherrif Hutton, York, often referred to a match with a horse team opposing a tractor and winning, but nine horses were used in relays of three.

On the small farm with insufficient, lame or worn-out horses, cutting corn was hell. We should always remember that horses in general have a far better time today than when they were the sole means of power. Then, they sometimes had to work when over-stressed or unsound. It was not deliberate cruelty, simply that the work had to be done and the harvest won somehow.

The scope for inequality and abuse in the old landlord/tenant system is ready fuel for its critics. They should remember the other side of the coin. Harry Rockliff told of how the owner of Beningbrough Hall kept spare teams of Shires on his home farm, so that a tenant could always be told 'Go to the home farm for a horse' if one of his own became lame at a busy time.

The Heaton Stud

One rather raw day in 1973, I went to a horse sale at a venue with an unlikely sounding name. It was New Bridge Chemical Works, Radcliffe, right in Lancashire's industrial heart. But the stud owners, J. & W. Whewell, were known wherever Shires were bred, their prefix Heaton was among the greats, and their stud groom Reg Nunn became a legend in his own lifetime.

In view of the Shire market in the preceding decade, there seemed an inordinate number of potential buyers at that sale. Or were they summoned, as to a wake, by mere inquisitiveness and the passing of a tradition?

The prices soon proved otherwise. I wish I could pin-point that sale as the turning point and say that I was struck by a Sherlock Holmes-type of insight that made the way ahead bright and clear. Alas, at the time it seemed no more than an encouraging flash in the pan. But it was a great sale.

The highlight was, of course, Heaton Majestic. Six times had he paraded at Peterborough in the gelding class, and six times had Reg Nunn walked up for the championship cup, the massive Majestic towering above him. There was not another gelding in the country even to approach Heaton Majestic.

The horse's sire was Crossfields Supreme, and his breeder J.B. Cooke, who later bred the Golden Guinea award winner Jim's Lucky Charm. The bay mare Lucky Charm was sired by Hillmoor Enterprise, out of a Lymm Sovereign mare, Jim's Chelsea. But as is the way with pedigrees, we are straying from our theme.

The Shire Horse Society held 25 gelding championships from 1948 to Whewell's last outing, in which time the Heaton stud took sixteen of them. From 1961 to Heaton Majestic's last appearance in 1972, the stud proved unbeatable, taking all 12.

Nor should anyone think that the competition was poor. Total Peterborough entries were rising slowly, but even in 1971 Heaton Majestic paraded in a strong class of 14 including the runner-up, Coward's St Vincent's Flash Lad, plus Harry Chambers' Swanland Dale Supreme, three brewery horses from Youngs and one from Courage's. Hull Brewery also entered Noble, and Arthur Wright from Warrington with the four-year-old Ned could never be discounted. The 1981 gelding class, four years old and upwards, had no more than 17 entries.

In the *Preston Guardian* during the 1943 season, that great heavy horse journalist Harry Holderness described the four-year-old champion Tabley Grey Duke 43496, by Powisland Bulwark out of Pilsdon Beauty:

He is a flash horse from whatever angle he is viewed, and his compactness and his close linking deceive one as to his height, but he is 17.1 hands for all that. Hard and steel-girdered, he is finished in the height of Shire fashion, and is wonderfully clean in his limbs, just as the champion of today ought to be. Further, he is beautifully topped and powerfully jointed.

Whewells again won the championship at Derby, under the auspices of the Shire Horse Society. Their horse was Bradford Diagram 43150, a six-year-old bay by Bradford Monogram. The bay Monogram was bred across the Pennines at Bradford by E. Patchett, and had three white legs and the near hind black. Diagram's dam was Margaret of Chippinghurst, who rose to fame rapidly as the only yearling filly to win the supreme female championship at the Shire Horse Show.

Harry Holderness wrote of Monogram in 1942:

A stalwart, carty horse which looks like being a getter of the deep draughter type, he is essentially modern in outline, and has a general balance and grandeur of outline which is most attractive. He is white socked, deep in front, set on frontal columns of infinite strength, not too long in the back, is sufficiently deep, and has a pair of levers which betoken his power. A notable feature is the remarkable flatness of his bone. Rippling with muscles of cable strength, he has an airy grace in his locomotion that is fascinating to behold in so heavy a horse. When he goes he seems to skim the turf, the while revealing the notable size of his mallet-like hoofs.

35 In 1967 it was quite a feat even to find this number of Shires, yet they were worked regularly at Young's Brewery, Wandsworth (*Fleet Fotos*)

Whewells did not achieve prominence through picking up unconsidered trifles. They bought the best, and advised others to do so. The Heaton Stud booklet reads: 'Students of pedigree should analyse the breeding of a stallion whose maternal lineage stands unsurpassed. Experimenting with chance-bred sires is a waste of time.'

The old stallion Pendley Harvester is the subject of this discourse in the booklet. He was foaled in 1927, and that year gained firsts at the leading Yorkshire shows, Wetherby, Malton, Withernsea, Church Fenton, Harrogate and Sherburn-in-Elmet, following up this early promise by leading his class in London as a yearling.

Another appreciative comment comes from Harry Holderness in 1942:

Pendley Harvester is undoubtedly a grand old gentleman and when he came out for his photograph looked amazingly fit for his advancing years. He showed off his paces to perfection, like the gallant veteran he is. He looks an old horse, of course, but he has preserved his virility to a surprising extent. He was first used when he was four years old, and has served more than a hundred mares a year since, leaving a high percentage in foal.

Pendley Harvester was a black with three white legs. He was bought by Whewells at the 1936 Pendley Stud sale for 380 guineas, or more than a hundred times the average farm man's weekly wage.

Another horse to cost the firm 380 guineas, though in 1942, was The Proctor 43672:

A sturdy bay with a blaze and three white legs, he is well grown for his age, and is noteworthy for the fine quality of his flat bone and for the really tremendous size of his foundations. His hair is in the right places and it is light and silky. There is ample heart room about him and he has that short back which is the prerequisite of the good stallion. Taken all round he looks a typical gelding getter of the Heaton type.

(Written in 1943).

And as the only true purpose of all Shire stallions is to get geldings of the Heaton type, these words are worth studying in depth.

7 The Grey and the Chestnut

Grey Shires

Grey is a colour that has waxed and waned throughout Shire history. Sir Walter Gilbey asserted that for a foal to be born grey, at least one of its parents must be grey. In 50 years he had never known the contrary. But in recent years a grey Shire has been foaled with a grey grandparent, neither of its parents being grey, so there is more hope than was suspected for the colour.

Grey has several shades, and also varies with age. It is not liked by those with little time to keep a horse clean, for as the animal ages, so does the owner! A smart dapple in a young horse may be almost white in 20 years, by which time its groom has less energy for keeping it smart. On the other hand, greys show dandruff and body dirt less than most other colours. Black tends to acquire a flecked appearance if the horse is warmed up, and as soon as the sweat dries it looks untidy. On the modern showfield horses do not exert themselves enough to sweat much, so that factor is of less account. There are at least five shades of grey: dappled, steel, iron, black and flea-bitten.

A few, a very few, Shires have been registered white. One was Erfyl Lady White 88451, the dam of Erfyl Lady Grey (Vol. 39 of the *Stud Book*).

The old grey mare is familiar through story and song, but not since 1957 has she won a Shire supreme championship. Success came early, however, for of eight grey mares to win the supreme accolade, the first was in 1882, only two years after the first Shire Horse Society Show at Islington.

The mare was Thursa, later numbered 1087. Not till Volume 13 of the *Stud Book* were females regarded as of sufficient significance to have an official numeral bestowed on them. Thursa was by Drayman 3058 by King Charles 1207, and out of a mare by that stallion. King Charles may be traced right back to Wiseman's Honest Tom 1060.

Thursa won her class and the senior championship the following year, when Sanders Spencer said that 'her fine movement, added to her immense substance, and good legs and feet, render her a formidable opponent in the show-ring'.

In 1886, the seven-year-old grey mare Bonny won the championship for Arthur Tomlinson of Stenson, Derbyshire. This mare was bought by William Arkwright of Sutton Scarsdale to help found his stud. He paid 500 guineas for her, which would have bought 20 acres of average land at the time. By today's scale that is in the £40,000 bracket.

The mare was renamed Scarsdale Bonny. She was by the grey Lincolnshire Lad II 1365, out of the black Depper, which Tomlinson also liked so much that he bought her. Bonny's two-year-old colt offspring, also a grey, came in the top ten out of 72 at the same show.

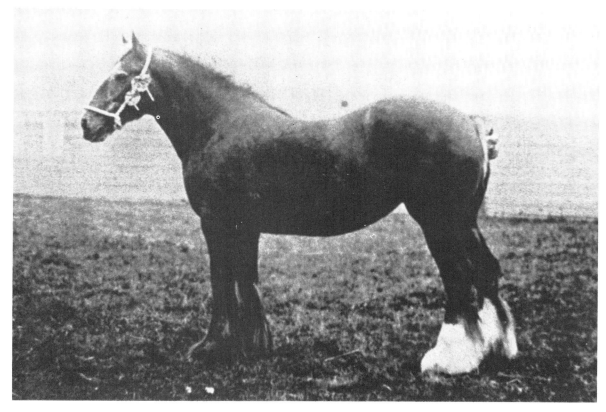

Lincolnshire Lad II remains in our study through Rokeby Fuchsia, champion mare in 1893 and 1894. Her sire was the roan Lincolnshire Boy, 3188, son of Lincolnshire Lad II, and her dam Lady Grey 15068. Would that she were around today – she had three more grey foals after Fuchsia, who was born in 1887.

Fuchsia was bred by W.H. and J. Spalton, Denby, Derbyshire, and won her championship for John Parnell of Rugby before being bought by A.J. Hollinton of Forty End, Enfield, the next year. She continued as both successful breeder and show animal, producing at least two grey fillies.

Our fourth champion grey mare also has Lincolnshire Lad II connections. She is Dunsmore Fuchsia, her sire Dunsmore Jameson 17972 being the great-grandson of Lincolnshire Lad II, and out of a mare by a son of Harold.

Dunsmore Fuchsia won in 1905 as a two-year-old. Another grey mare, the eight-year-old Shelford Pax 26856, stood reserve to her, and was of the same bloodline, her grandsire, Lincolnshire Lad II, being the founder.

In 1907, Dunsmore Fuchsia's owner P.A. Muntz held a highly successful sale in which 52 Shires averaged £149, the best price of the year. Fuchsia went to Devon, to William Whitley, and though shown she never regained her former status.

Another great grey was Sussex Bluegown, owned by the Forshaws at Carlton-on-Trent. She did not comply with breeding regulations for her class, introduced in 1905, and so was not regarded as the official 1906 champion. She has, however, passed on her wonderful qualities to the

36 Dunsmore Fuchsia was a grey, foaled in 1903 and bought at the 1907 Dunsmore sale for 520 guineas, following a string of firsts and championships

present day: her great-grandson was the grey March King 34955, foaled in 1916, who sired Ponton Pioneer (of whom more later).

Of all the grey female champions, the most publicized and probably the greatest was Erfyl Lady Grey. She won the supreme female championships at Islington in 1924, 1925 and 1926.

A.G. Holland, in Vesey Fitzgerald's *Book of the Horse*, writes:

Many good judges consider that the best of all Shire mares seen out was that great winner Erfyl Lady Grey by Moors Kitchener. Judges could not fault her, she was as near perfection as possible. Thrice female champion in London, and twice at the Royal Show, Erfyl Lady Grey was possessed of great substance, wonderful breed character, conformation and activity, yet with all she had great feminine quality. At her last show in London she scaled 22¼cwt, and for the sake of records we give her measurements. These were: Height, 17 hands 1½ins; girth, 9ft; forearm, 23½ins; hind thighs, 22½ins; bone, 12½ins below knee; bone, 13ins below hock; feet (fore), 9ins across bare foot. A glorious type of mare in every way.

Among the great greys of the early 1900s were Monks Polly and Darling. The latter stood 17.3 hands high, and was long and massive in proportion. The dam of Lymm Grey, Darling won firsts at leading county shows from 1904, when she was a six-year-old. Lymm Grey won at the Lincoln Royal Show in 1907, and his amount of bone would be welcome in a stallion today.

Monks Polly was foaled a year later, and was bred by Geoffrey Wainwright, of Monks Heath, Chelford, Cheshire. After a spell in the Intake Stud at Sheffield she was bought by Earl Beauchamp and stabled at Madresfield Court, Malvern. She had a string of show successes, and was dam of the famous Starborough Chief 21898.

In 1937 the grey Shire Marden Daphne gained the London Shire Show championship as a three-year-old. She won her class, the junior championship, and beat the four-year-old Leek Beauty for the supreme championship.

Harry Holderness said of her: 'Since last year Daphne has done her best, attained plenty of range and scale, and furnished on modern lines. Like so many greys, she wears her head aloft, sweeps the tan with a free and buoyant stride, and keeps her flat hocks together.'

In 1938 she lost the championship to Leek Beauty, and her black colt foal, Marden Luck, born two years later, seems to be the only one in the *Stud Book*.

Another champion grey female was Crimwell Quality. Her great-grandsire was Ponton Pioneer 38453, owned by William Todd of Little Ponton Grange, Grantham. His two aims were to breed cleaner-legged, more active Shires, and to breed greys. Ponton Pioneer helped fulfil both ambitions.

There is an interesting story about Pioneer. When his portrait was being painted by Fred Thurlby the horse took apparent exception to the work and put a giant hoof through the canvas! The repair may be seen to this day at John Porter's Grantham home.

Ponton Pioneer was by March King. That stallion was great grandsire of Lymm Grey King, two of whose offspring were Bradgate Lady Grey and the black Lymm Winnie, who were next in line to Crimwell Quality when she won the Shire Horse Society championship at Derby Market in 1943. She was unbeaten at the 1947, '48 and '49 Society shows.

The last of the champion grey females to date was Creswell Grey Princess, who in 1956 won for Fred Moss, of Creswell Farm, Betchton, Rode Heath,

Stoke. Her ancestry is typical of a number of farm-reared horses kept primarily to provide the work force, but well bred to the best sires available.

Creswell Grey Princess may be traced along a strain of Shire mares in the ownership of the Roberts family in Derbyshire which probably goes back to the 1860s at least.

Marmion II, Norbury Menstrel, Harborough Nulli Secundus and Carlton Grey Kingmaker are among the illustrious names figuring in Grey Princess's pedigree. Her sire was the thickset Newton Fields Ambassador, a dark bay bred to Kirkland Mimic. Her one registered offspring was the brown Cresswell Princess Grace by Minoan, foaled in the year after the championship victory of 1956.

The glut of grey Shires in the 1940s came largely from Ponton Pioneer and Grey King Carlton, the two most important, but separate, lines derived from March King.

Chestnuts

All Suffolks are chesnut – spelt in that breed without the central 't' – but the Shire Horse Society does not welcome the colour.

The Society scale of breed points specifically bars chestnut stallions, and has done since 1972. 'He should not be roan or chestnut' it says emphatically. Mares and geldings may be roan or chestnut, but the obvious official attitude is to try and breed out these colours.

A roan Shire might well be mistaken for a Clyde, but the prejudice against chestnut has less validity. The colour has roots in the breed's early history, and a number of notable winners have been of that colour.

In the first Shire Horse Society Show at Islington in 1880, three of the five stallion classes were won by chestnuts, against two by bays. In the five-year-old and upwards stallion class, the winner was Champion 440, who was then 13. The horse had already won £1,300 in prize money, at 74 different shows. He was owned by the Stand Stud Company, Manchester, and bred by Thomas Stokes at Caldecott, Uppingham, Rutland, in the heart of Shire country.

Champion's sire was Champion 413, that stallion also being his maternal grandsire. He was a roan, foaled in 1852 at Desborough, Northamptonshire, and was one of 88 stallions named Champion listed in the first four volumes of the *Stud Book*. That there were also 15 Champion of Englands may be taken as a reflection of the optimism of that age!

Other chestnut winners at Islington 1880 were the three-year-old Rutland Champion and the yearling Coming Wonder. The former was sired by Champion 441, owned by Thomas Stokes, breeder of Champion 440, and the grandsire was Champion 413 mentioned above. Coming Wonder's sire was England's Wonder 761 (The Old Strawberry).

In 1884 a chestnut won the supreme female championship. She was Czarina, a three-year-old by the bay Helmdon's Emperor. She was then described as 'a wonder for her age; immense substance, depth of rib, length of quarter, flat bone, fine quality of hair, good feet, and for so heavy a filly, fine action which render her an animal in every way fitted to receive honours as a champion female of the Shire breed.'

Czarina's owner was the Hon. Edward Coke, president of the Society in 1881. All his Shires registered at Longford Hall, Derby, had names beginning with the letter C.

Until 1900, most Shire shows listed chestnuts among the winners. In 1885 Royal Sandys was first in the big stallion class, and he was let for £500, so obviously many farmers valued chestnut at that time.

The 1881 Volume II of the *Stud Book* lists 138 stallions, of which 23, or 16 per cent, were chestnut. In this same Volume II, 75, or $14\frac{1}{2}$ per cent of the 516 mares were chestnut. There were fewer than eight grey stallions and 40 grey mares – 6 and 7.7 per cent respectively.

The last time a chestnut stallion won a first at a Shire Horse Society annual show was in 1889. This was a three-year-old, RR6300 by MM3205, and described as 'handsome, stylish and free-moving'. MM3205 was a bay, as was his dam Woodhouse's Bess, but the latter's sire was the chestnut Sir Colin, foaled 1869.

Chestnuts were accepted in the best studs in the land until 1900, and the reason for their decline is not easy to ascertain. But the most famous chestnut was still to be foaled. Dunsmore Chessie was bought by P.A. Muntz, Dunsmore, Rugby, and on his death soon afterwards the filly was taken over by the former stud manager Thomas Ewart. She won her London class as a two-year-old, and was sold for £588 the next year, topping the entry of 161. Her new owner was Sir Walpole Greenwell of Marden Park. At the Liverpool Royal she again won her class, and again stood reserve to Forest Princess in the championship.

After more successes at leading shows, Dunsmore Chessie came into her own as a four-year-old, winning the supreme female championship in 1912. She repeated this feat in 1913, but those who expected the colour's continued success to be reflected in the coats of the next generation were disappointed. Her name was more influential: a large number of Chessies were around after 1911.

The last chestnut to win a first at the London Shire Show was the gelding Punch in 1921. In 1920 the four-year-old chestnut Dogdyke Premier had won the gelding championship, with the three-year-old Punch as reserve. But in 1925 Mann, Crossman and Paulin Ltd gained reserve for the best working team – and they were Shire geldings.

Perhaps the brewers, who have done so much to save the breed, might now re-introduce the chestnut colour and fight for its acceptance. It would be a worthy and popular aim.

Yet there is still hope – and an interesting tail piece to the story. At the 1978 Centenary Show, the second prize yearling filly was Churchill Pride 140768. She is registered in Volume 101 of the *Stud Book* as a chestnut. One of the judges commented: 'Who's she by? The Minstrel?' The Minstrel was a very flashy chestnut who won the 1977 Derby!

8 The Society's Second Century

At the beginning of its second century, the Shire Horse Society is a well-organized body. This fact was reflected in the award of the M.B.E. to its Secretary, Roy Bird, one of the hardest working and most outward-looking livestock secretaries in a profession noted for dedication and action.

The Society is a registered charity limited by guarantee. It is governed by a council of 36 elected representatives, with all Past Presidents serving as *ex-officio* members. Twelve members of Council retire by rotation each year, and are eligible for re-election. The Society has enjoyed royal patronage since its inception, and Her Majesty Queen Elizabeth II is the fifth Royal Patron and the third Royal President.

The Shire Horse Society is based at the East of England Showground, Peterborough, PE2 0XE. Administration includes organization of the National Spring Show, schedule entries, catalogues, the Stallion Premium Scheme, promotional activities and all *Stud Book* entries. Affiliated societies come in for special consideration, and are awarded special prizes and helped with classifications. The export of Shire horses is also dealt with through the Society.

38 Peterborough entries are now so numerous that a second ring must be brought into operation (*Audrey Hart*)

Society membership is open to everyone with an interest in Shire horses. Life membership costs £100, while joint membership including two badges for the Spring Show costs £10 per year.

The main object of the Society is the promotion and improvement of the breed of Shire horses.

Annual Show

The National Spring Show date has been moved from late March to early April and back again, and from Wednesday to Saturday. There are frequent requests for a later date, in the hope of warmer weather, but the allocation of premiums and the parade of stallions is an important part of the show. A May or June show date would mean their absence at stud.

It is also argued that staging show classes just before the breeding season encourages stallion owners to over-feed their horses, to the detriment of breeding qualities. The Spring Show was certainly dogged by some foul weather in the 1970s, for the fenland winds at that time of year have to be felt to be believed.

Consequently, some older members who love Shires simply cannot face the cold. Yet at no other event is there such an array of stallions, especially senior stallions, and I wonder whether the provision of temporary, warm viewing accommodation is a feasible proposition. Those who now feel the cold worst are among the breed stalwarts who kept the Shire in being when everything seemed against it.

The Society's annual dinner is held on the evening before the show. Its reception by members has been as mixed as the venues tried, but the Shire Horse Society has been most fortunate in its choice of clerical speakers at these events. Each has been in the top bracket as an informed entertainer.

39 An experienced observer of the summer show scene. (*Audrey Hart*)

Publications

Two or three newsletters are sent out to members annually. Copies of the Annual Report and Accounts are also available free. A most useful list of members was included in the centenary catalogue, real value at £1. The list of breeders is published annually, and contains the names of premium stallion owners and local hiring societies.

Each year the growing list of shows at which Shire horses are exhibited is published, free. It is an essential to every Shire enthusiast. Application forms for shows to affiliate to the Society are supplied.

An official panel of judges has been compiled, and the list of names is invaluable to show secretaries. There are also guide notes for judges.

There is a breed chart showing points of conformation, and a descriptive leaflet including general information. A plaiting card gives advice on plaiting for the show ring.

The annual *Stud Book* is in loose leaf form, and certainly has its critics. Many much poorer societies produce a bound volume, while the Shire Horse Society merely provides loose leaves held together with metal studs.

Purchase of Horses

Potential Shire buyers must be absolutely certain that they are buying registered animals. If there is doubt, a telephone call to the office, with the name and description of the horse and the name of the vendor will immediately ascertain whether the horse in question is a registered pedigree Shire, or whether it is in the Grading Register. If it is an unregistered foal, the eligibility for registration can be checked.

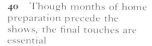

40 Though months of home preparation precede the shows, the final touches are essential

Export

The Shire Horse Society gives a valuable service to buyers from abroad. Members of the Editing Committee will accompany potential purchasers to look at and advise on horses for sale, and expenses only are charged.

Though geldings do not need export certificates, all other classes of Shires do. The Society will act as stakeholder, and will arrange insurance, transport and shipping. A fee is payable for this comprehensive service, and the vendor is responsible for the cost of the export certificate.

Generally speaking, the price of the horse is agreed, and that price is the amount paid to the vendor. The buyer is also responsible for all tests and

41 Hillmoor Enterprise, champion stallion at the Peterborough show in 1975 (*Lee Weatherley*)

42 General view of the Royal Show. A Percheron 'four' stands behind the free-moving Shires in the foreground. The next two teams are 'unicorns' of Shires, with one lead horse and two wheelers. The farthest team are Suffolks. (*Audrey Hart*)

veterinary surgeon's fees, for insurance and for transport from the farm to the point of embarkation, and for the air or sea freight.

USA air freight, even for a young horse, may well exceed £1,000. Rates depend on weight, so there is a temptation to take a young, unproven animal, which makes it imperative that it is of sound pedigree.

With such a high freight charge however, there is little point in economizing in the choice of animal, and yearling colts and fillies of a quality suitable for export fetch from £1,000 to £5,000. Foals fetch somewhat less, and mature breeding horses, both mares and stallions, range from £2,000 to £10,000.

These prices depend on the quality, colour and pedigree of the animals. Scarcity adds value, and, for instance, anyone seeking a matched six-in-hand of bay geldings would be difficult to fit up. Nor are the lovely greys easy to find.

The Shire Horse Society member who accompanies would-be buyers acts purely in an advisory capacity. Neither he nor the Society can be held in any way responsible if the deal turns out to be unsatisfactory.

Though photographs are useful, they are only a guide, and the buyer is well advised either to see the horse in person, or to engage a reliable horseman to act for him.

If the would-be purchaser cannot visit the United Kingdom, and wants the Shire Horse Society to conduct his business for him, details required are:

1 Exact details of the horses required: age, colour, markings if any, sex and any particular breed line.

43 1980 champion Ladbrook Aristocrat (*Lee Weatherley*)

2 An indication as to whether the Shires should be top quality show animals themselves, or good horses capable of breeding the best.

3 Maximum price.

4 If a deal is made, a deposit of half the sale value is required, payable to the Society. This enables the final arrangements to be made. Transport, insurance and shipping will be arranged, and the deposit is held by the Society until full payment is received. This must be in the hands of the Society before the horse leaves the farm.

5 Payment should be by banker's draft wherever possible. If by cheque, at least 14 days must be allowed for clearance.

Horserace Betting Levy Board

One positive factor in the heavy-horse resurgence has been the interest and financial help of the Horserace Betting Levy Board. Each heavy-horse breed society is dealt with independently, and the Shire Horse Society acknowledges its debt to the Board, and has received by far the largest sum. This is due to greater numbers, but also doubtless to the drive and flair with which its case was presented.

The Society is pledged to apply this money strictly in accordance with the Board's wishes to improve the breed of Shire horses. In 1980, the grant was £20,000, and as the Society contributed £4,000, the total sum available in the Stallion Premium account was £24,000.

Below

44 Set piece of Shires and grooms at the Bisquit Cognac Shire Horse of the Year Show

45 Mr W.S. Innes with his four-year-old gelding Ty Fry Hiawatha, by Woodhouse Pioneer out of Theale Ann

46 High Spirits from Decoy Royal Surprise. G.T. Ward & Sons' mare went on to win the Bisquit Cognac Shire Horse of the Year Championship in 1980

The object of the Stallion Premium Scheme is to provide a Shire stallion of approved type within reach of every breeder in Great Britain. Previously, the best market for males, limited though it was, had been as matched geldings in brewery teams. Inevitably this resulted in some excellent horses being castrated, and the Stallion Premium Scheme sought to redress the balance.

By the early 1980s, the scheme had succeeded to the extent that some thinking breeders considered that the swing had gone too far. A variable scale of premiums of up to £400 for mature stallions enticed owners of young colts to gain cash while it was going, so quality geldings became in short supply.

The ultimate object of Shire breeding is, or should be, the production of geldings capable of moving massive loads. On one of Forshaw's stud cards was the slogan: 'Weight Moves Weight – Keep the Lorry in View.' As more and more firms turn to heavy horses for local deliveries, there should be more financial incentive to rear and train geldings capable of the work. Or so the rearers feel.

Most premiums are given at the Spring Show at Peterborough. A few older stallions may be inspected at home, and saved the long journey. Horserace Betting Levy Board representatives who regularly attend the Spring Show must indeed feel gratified by the marvellous display of stallions gathered together.

9 The Shire at Work

Farm Machinery

The farmer and stockbreeder breeds his animals to meet the needs of the time. We have seen how the medieval Great Horse was bred, so that he could carry the weight of a man in armour. Heavy horses were imported from the Continent, and the most suitable of their offspring selected.

Royal decrees then came into force, forbidding the use of small or pony stallions in certain areas. The decrees were not sufficiently precise geographically, for to seek to displace small horses in upland districts was impractical. The heavy horse cannot fulfil its growth potential on exposed rough grazing, where altitude brings the driving winds and heavy rains.

Although the ox was the chief source of draught power until the nineteenth century, it is noteworthy that most early farm machine prototypes were horse-drawn.

In the eighteenth century, three major developments were made, in drilling, ploughing and threshing. Jethro Tull's seed drill and horse hoe set the scene, for the one was dependent on the other for effective use. We know from our own times that the single-row horse hoe or scruffler does not

48 A four-horse hitch is necessary for the binder on Devon hills. The Devon Shire Horse Farm Centre, Yealmpton, carries out normal farming operations with the teams. In 1981 a quarter of a million visitors saw the Shires. (*Devon Shire Horse Farm Centre*)

49 Ploughing near Duggleby on the Wolds, from a painting by Charles Simpson R.I. Shires were almost universal on these arable uplands, where the soil might be so thin that, in the words of one old horseman, 'in some places you could bury your plough point and in some places you couldn't'

require great strength to haul it, but that a steady animal is essential. This steadiness is gained partly through the horse being well on top of its job, meaning that it does not have to swing from side to side to gain purchase, but walks away easily and in a straight line. The horse must be placid by nature; when 'blood' horses (Thoroughbreds) were tried on the land in World War Two, it was found that there were a number of farm jobs to which they were quite unsuited, though their strength was adequate.

Even at the end of the 'First Horse Age', many elderly Shires were semi-retired, doing such work as drilling turnips and scruffling them the first time over. On the precision given to such tasks depends much of the success of later cleaning operations.

The plough has remained a basic farm implement ever since its invention. The heavy old wooden ploughs required a team of up to eight or even 12 oxen and two drivers. A prolonged midday break was required, as oxen needed time not only to eat but to chew the cud.

The earliest light ploughs came from Holland, and were used chiefly in East Anglia. In 1655 R. Child wrote *A Large Letter* to M. Samuel Hartlib, mentioning the Norfolk practice of ploughing with two horses only. In Ireland farmers yoked their horses by the tails, a cruel and inefficient practice.

In the 1790s Coke of Norfolk sent a Norfolk plough, a ploughman and a pair of horses into Gloucestershire, where two men, a boy and a team of six horses were traditionally employed in ploughing. Yet 20 years passed before neighbouring farmers profited from the lesson.

We may assume that the horses were of the Old English cart horse type, and Volume I of the *Stud Book*, 1879, takes us towards that era with its retrospective entries.

As the nineteenth century dawned, horses had ousted oxen almost completely from plough teams. Two other factors aided the horse's output: the Industrial Revolution brought a spread of standardized iron ploughs, with lighter draught, and the dynamometer was invented.

The latter, placed between plough and team, enabled the draught to be calculated. The effect of a skim coulter or shorter mouldboard could be assessed accurately rather than guessed. The dynamometer proved whether or not the supposed superiority of different types of share or mouldboard was a matter of tradition rather than fact. Ransomes of Suffolk used the dynamometer, and by 1843 could claim that the firm employed almost 1,000 craftsmen, and that 300 types of plough for use at home and abroad were made.

Ransomes had also recently introduced the chilled iron share. Its harder working surface was kept sharp by the quicker wearing of the softer inner edge.

Such were the diverse factors affecting the working horse's development. There were legal influences, too. Short term tenancies stifled innovation, for a man could be turned off the holding he had striven to improve, with never a penny's compensation. Ultra-conservative tradition was encouraged by poor communications and isolated villages.

One of the first machines to require strong, quick-stepping horses was the reaper. Four reapers were patented before 1828, one of which was made by James Smith and was inspected at work by a committee of the Highland and Agricultural Society in 1815. This committee reported so favourably as to

50 Catching a pair of Shires for work on a farm near Scarborough

declare the machine 'next to the plough itself, the most valuable invention that has occurred in the annals of husbandry'.

Smith's reaper failed on a farm scale. The sickle versus the scythe remained the harvest debate.

The son of an Angus farmer, Patrick Bell, made the first successful reaping machine in 1828. He foresaw the increasing difficulties of assembling an adequate harvest gang, and gained his idea from a pair of garden shears sticking in the garden hedge. The cutting-machine was first tested in a barn, with corn stalks stuck into soil brought in for the purpose. Not surprisingly, its first field trial took place when the rest of the farm staff were safely in bed.

Bell's reaper may be seen in its entirety in the Science Museum, Kensington, London. That admirable museum is worth a horseman's visit to see this implement alone, though it has many other treasures. The reaper was pushed rather than pulled, being in that way the fore-runner of the self-propelled combine, and would have avoided the need to 'open out' a field with the scythe before using the binder.

A writer at the time estimated that the reaper could save one million pounds a year over Britain as a whole. Its extensive use would have called for more and better horses. But in the next four years only ten machines were made, though it is possible that Bell's machine aided American inventors.

Among these was Cyrus McCormick. He was only seven when he saw a machine pushed from behind by two horses, which failed to cut corn and made his father-inventor the butt of the American countryside's jokes. But when he was aged 22, Cyrus yoked a horse to his own reaper, and it worked.

This was the start of mechanical reaping, and of prairie farming, for the McCormicks moved to the embryo Chicago, the site of so much farming

progress. The reaper was shown in trials before judges at the Great Exhibition at Crystal Palace in 1851, and caused a sensation. Bell's machine was resurrected, and more trials followed. Both machines proved practical, but while Bell reaped esteem and £1,000 from the Highland and Agricultural Society, the McCormicks were to develop into the International Harvester Company and turn out thousands of machines a week by the end of the century.

McCormick reapers were still renowned for light draught as long as British horses pulled them. They were high-geared, so a pair moving at a spanking walk made easier progress than two sluggards.

Later nineteenth-century breeders set out to meet the demand for suitable teams. The horse was roused from his summer holiday; when grass and corn were mown by scythe and turned and tended by hand, the horses were concerned only with leading the harvest home. Now they had to cut the grass, and the corn, though the latter was still bound by hand.

The first reapers left a continuous swathe. Then a manual delivery system left the corn in sheaf sizes that still had to be bound by hand. Later a self-delivery and then a side-delivery machine came, but five men had to work hard to keep up with the machine.

The knotter was tried at the Royal Show of 1877. It influenced Shire breeding at home, for its logical development in the self-binder called for large teams of powerful horses. In 1878 William Deering started production of the world's first successful harvester-binding machine incorporating a twine-fibre knotting mechanism for bundling sheaves, which enabled prairie farmers to engulf Britain with shiploads of cheap grain. Britain's farming boom, when large-scale tenants lived like gentlemen, was over.

English and Welsh farm staffs could cope with the rows of sheaves deposited by the self-binder. They were stooked neatly in pairs, four or five

52 The McCormick reaper of 1847, on which seats were placed for the driver and the raker. The reaper sails are necessary to cause the cut corn to drop backwards onto the slatted platform

53 The Shire pair and the trace horse are walking with a self-binder in a fine crop of wheat. The straw looks ideal for thatching, whereas the modern combine pulverizes it (*International Harvester*)

pairs to the stook, led home by cart and waggon and Shire, and stacked and thatched neatly to give an artist's dream. Then in winter the threshing machine arrived, in the early days drawn by horse teams, and a supply of fresh oats and straw was assured.

The Americans had no use for by-products, and no labour to stook the endless acres. They and the Australians soon developed the combine harvester which necessitated really big teams of horses or mules. In 1914 the International Harvester Company started production in America of combines, then known as 'harvester threshers'.

Whole books have been devoted to the craftsman-built carts and waggons that were part of the rural scene until just after World War Two. The best types for each district were discovered – and adhered to. Pneumatic tyres brought some improvement on hard roads, though not always in difficult conditions such as when the first thaw touched hard frozen ground. Iron tyres gripped far better in those conditions.

The latest development is the hitch cart, designed primarily to enable many tractor-drawn implements to be pulled by horses without the need for expensive conversions. Obvious applications include chain harrows, cultivators, rollers and two-wheeled trailers.

The hitch cart as made by Pinney is of box-section steel, with roller-

bearing hubs, and six-ply heavy duty pneumatic tyres on 16-inch wheels. Its stability and quiet running also make it an ideal exercising and breaking vehicle. The basic specification includes a pressed steel frame, a weldmesh platform and a hand rail. A two-jaw towing hitch taking a wide range of machinery is welded close to the wheel centre line, while there is a movable attachment point for the draft bars, to allow either two or three horses abreast. Shafts can be fitted for one-horse jobs.

Many readers will be familiar with Youatt's oft-reprinted book *The Horse*. Most editions are concluded by 'A Treatise on Draught', but in few is the author's name added to that section. It was in fact Brunel, the world-famous engineer, and anyone concerned with modern design of horse-drawn vehicles or implements would be well repaid by detailed study of Brunel's chapter.

Local Traditions

During the working horse's heyday, the Shire predominated over much of England and Wales. In Cumberland Clydesdales were as formidable as any bred north of the Border, while Durham and Northumberland housed famous studs of the Scottish breed; Clydesdales or Clydesdale-type

54 Cutting grass. The lever enables the reciprocating knife to be 'jacked up' when cornering. Grass mowing can be done early in the morning, despite dew, but corn can only be cut during the heat of the day when it is dry. (*International Harvester*)

provided most of the power on their lowland farms. On the upland farms, Dales and Fell ponies served every purpose from making hay to pulling the trap to chapel or market. Often they were crossed with a heavier breed, to little advantage.

In a broad band across Westmorland and the North Riding, Shire and Clyde merged. Stallions of both breeds travelled. Farm men argued, often ferociously, about their respective merits. But the differences among the unregistered stock were minimal.

A line from Kendal, Westmorland, through the northern edge of the Vale of York to Whitby on the east coast may be taken as the approximate dividing line between Shire and Clydesdale. In the eastern counties, the Suffolk breed made its influence felt, as did the Percheron after World War One. In Wales there were and are several notable Shire studs, with the native Welsh Cob filling the same role on upland farms as the Dales and Fell on the Pennines. In the south-west, ponies were similarly used on the smaller, steeper fields.

Each heavy-horse district developed its own methods and traditions in those days of slow and limited communications. None was more distinctive than the Yorkshire Wolds, that area of chalk and limestone upland starting close to the North Sea, and bounded by Malton and Ryedale to the north and the great plain of Holderness to the south, where in the nineteenth century there was a breed of cart horse known as the Holderness Black.

The Horsemen

The Wolds was an area of large farms. They had been laid out by the Sykes family and others from open sheepwalk, with a skill and forethought sadly absent in today's professionally qualified planners. The homesteads, snug in their U-shaped shelterbelts backed to the North Sea, led out onto large square or rectangular fields cut by dry dales.

In these grassy dales the horses summered. In winter they munched clover hay, for a quarter of the farm was 'seeds', another quarter being sown with oats, a proportion of which was fed to the teams.

Single men formed the bulk of the staffs, for cottages were few, and they boarded either with the farmer or the foreman. The regime under which they lived was almost military in character.

The foreman was in charge of the day to day schedule, and of the 'Tommy Owts', as the hand workers were termed. Leading the horsemen was the waggoner, invariably known as 'Wag', followed by the first horseman, second horseman, third horseman or 'thoddy', and so on down the line of, perhaps, ten or more employees.

If the farmer saw a man doing a job wrongly, he would never say so directly. He would mention it to the foreman, who would speak to the waggoner, and soon the miscreant learned of his mistake in no uncertain manner.

Before World War One, men worked from 6a.m. till 6p.m. in the fields. There were no free Saturday afternoons, and Good Friday was spent digging and planting the farm garden. On Sundays the gangs of horsemen walked from one farm to another, criticizing the straightness of the furrows, turnip rows or 'seam rows' of corn. Anyone whose load of corn or hay slipped off, 'teamed' or 'pigged', as they would say, was the butt of jokes for weeks.

In my boyhood days in the Vale of York I met a number of former Wolds

horsemen, and all bore a mark of slightly superior distinction. They told how on misty mornings they would set off to find their horses, some one way, some another, in a hundred-acre dale. There might be 30 or 40 horses, all instinctively herded into one area, and the finders shouted to warn their mates, slipped halters onto the quietest horses, and led the lot into the stables.

The horses were tied up, and collars and traces or saddles slipped on before the horsemen breakfasted. That meal was not an occasion for ceremony. It is part of Wolds folklore that if the breakfast call came when you had the horse's collar over its head in the upside down position, by the time you had swung it round you were too late for the meal!

A prince among the Wolds farms was Cowlam, with its church in the stackyard and its fields a mile long. Working with Shires there entailed hanging one's 'bait bag' on the horse's hames, as it would be ''lowance time' or 'ten o'clocks' when the far side was reached.

In one dry harvest the farmer hung a flag outside his bedroom window. If it was dry early in the morning, he called his staff immediately. If damp, they had an extra hour of blissful sleep. The lads devised the idea of dipping the flag in a bucket of water after the boss had gone to bed!

One of the most monotonous horse jobs was 'scruffling' or side-hoeing turnips. The scruffler was a single-row iron-toothed implement driven between the rows of turnips and, after the first time over, requiring little skill. So large were the Wolds fields that by the time a pair of horsemen had finished at one side, the weeds had grown sufficiently to start again on the other. 'Them lads was sick of scruffling,' said one horseman of two chaps who spent virtually all of one summer in the same field.

Each horseman was in charge of two Shires. He took one scruffling in the morning, from 6a.m. till noon, and the other in the afternoon, till 6p.m. So

55 The great number of workers on the land is shown in this haymaking scene. The scene is the north of England, and the semi-peaked collars are typical of Durham and Northumberland. The horses in the hay rakes are not true Shires; they are probably a mixture of Shire, Clydesdale and Dales pony. As machines grew bigger, many Fell and Dales ponies were crossed with Shire or Clydesdale stallions, to the detriment of the pony breeds. (*Beamish North of England Open Air Museum*)

77

56 The hay loader in operation: start (top) and finish. The hay loader for two horses in tandem was yoked behind a large cart. The apparatus was driven along a swathe, and a strong team was needed as the machine had to be worked through gears driven from the land wheels

the horses had a change, and walked away as fresh as paint. 'No one ever thought of giving the *men* a rest,' was the teller's rejoinder.

One very wet and dismal harvest, the farmer was at his wits' end to provide work for his horsemen. Day after day the heavens opened, and every loose box had been cleaned out and whitewashed, the main wet-day job at that time. In despair he gave his staff half-a-crown ($12\frac{1}{2}$p) each to go to Scarborough. They set off rejoicing, and the next day the sun shone, and continued until harvest home.

Another Woldsman used nothing except black Shires, and stamped a number on the hoof of each. He spent much of his time scouring England for suitable replacements.

The horsemen's lives revolved around their charges. Before work the horses were fed, curry-combed and harnessed. Every evening they were groomed again, and given an extra feed late on. Winter evenings were often spent in the warm stable, with snorting, stamping of ironshod feet and pulling of hay as constant accompaniment. The characteristics of every Shire in the stable were known down to the minutest detail.

In the churchyard at Sledmere is a monument to the Wolds Waggoners. They were raised by the squire and fitted into army routine very readily after the type of discipline to which they had been subjected before 1914.

Herbert Day, who worked on the Wolds at that time, knew of only one farm where Clydesdales were kept. All the rest had Shires. We may imagine the 'ribbing' that the outnumbered Clydesdale horsemen suffered at the hands of the Shire lads!

A Harvest in the 1940s

During the first half of the present century, heavy-horse work in Britain changed little. The single-furrow plough, sets of straight-tined and chisel-toothed harrows, rollers, scrufflers, corn and root drills, reapers, horse rakes and sweeps, self-binders and carts and waggons provided a basis by which any farm could be worked.

In the inter-war depression of the 1920s and '30s, few farmers had money to risk on innovations. With wages at around 32 shillings (£1.60) a week, there was little incentive to cut down staff, especially when a displaced man was a neighbour in a close-knit village community. When the manager of a large estate said to the owner: 'We can do without some of these men,' the reply was: 'Yes, but can they do without us?'.

The last 'all horse' harvest in which I took part was in 1949. It was a fitting finale, so different from some of the rain-soaked harvests experienced as a school boy. It differed only in detail from hundreds of such harvests on the larger arable farms of Britain over half a century.

It was a golden year. Crops were good, the sun shone from morning till night, and the ground was firm enough to carry the self-binder and the 'draughts' or carts and rullies.

With all the corn cut and stooked, we set about leading it home. The level Vale of York stubble rustled underfoot, and crunched beneath the cart wheels as we made our way through blackberry-edged gateways to the ruler-straight rows of stooks.

There were seven of us, with two carts and two single-horse rullies. Two men, or a man and a girl, built the stack, four were in charge of a horse apiece, and one man forked in the field.

The essence of the system was to 'keep the forker going'. As long as he was pitching sheaves non-stop from the lines of stooks, progress was being made, so the rest had to fit in as best they could. As soon as the next 'draught' appeared in the field, the man loading would 'fill up' by laying sheaves lengthways to bind the rest, by which time the empty cart or waggon had trundled across the white stubble, and the forker began to pitch sheaves into it almost without ceasing.

I was driving Beauty, a Shire bred by one of the registered stallions that travelled the district each spring. Even as I drove across the field, the cart in

57 Visitors gladly pay to help with the harvest at the Devon Shire Horse Farm Centre! Traditional iron-tyred carts are being used. (*Devon Shire Horse Farm Centre*)

front was filled up and ready to go, perhaps with only two courses of sheaves on. But woe betide anyone who had not returned by the time the previous load had been topped out to maximum capacity.

The cart body was filled with sheaves laid lengthways, then the shelvings or extended wooden framework was covered with sheaves butt-end outwards. The butt or 'arse' end of each sheaf was thicker than the head, where the ears of corn lay, and so the load could be tapered inwards for safety.

After this first 'square course', sheaves were laid lengthways in a 'filling' or 'shipping' course. Between each pair of stooks the Shire ambled forward on command, far easier and pleasanter than hopping on and off a noisy, vibrating tractor polluting the air with its fumes.

Once the cart was being loaded, the forker was in charge of the horse. He it was who uttered the warning 'Hold fast', which many Shires came to recognize as an indication that a move was required. If they veered left or

58 The Shire mare Melody of the placid eye. She looks completely trustworthy even with this small boy. (*Western Morning News Co. Ltd*)

59 Modern working Shires as depicted by the Misses E.M. and D.M. Alderson, Darlington. Brought up with horses, the artists do not need to research harness and yoking; they know every detail because they have linked the chains and led the horses back to the stable

right they were corrected with 'Gee back' or 'Arve'. Then the command 'Whoa!' was given when they were strategically placed for the next pair of stooks, but with their heads far enough from a stook to discourage thieving.

Returning to the stackyard, the horseman walked by his horse's head. Steering alongside the stack, he jumped onto his load and began to 'team', or unload, two sheaves at a time and steady. If sheaves were pitched up anyhow and in a direction that did not suit the stacker, they were liable to come tumbling down again, doubling the work. So we soon learnt.

Beauty and most of the others were home-bred, and of a family that was 'bull-headed' or rather stupid. An intelligent horse is a tremendous asset at work, and modern Shire breeders should give more consideration to this aspect. Those other working animals, the Border Collies, are selected on ability to work rather than on good looks.

Even ability to pull is seldom measured in the modern Shire. There are a few pulling competitions in Britain, but nothing like so many as in North America, and the few obstacle competitions reflect the driver's skill as much as the manoeuvrability of the horses.

Temperament and intelligence are extremely difficult to tabulate. Breeding for them is far more complex than selecting for black body colour and four white socks. It is an aspect that ought to be tackled, one reason being that horsemen and women of the 1980s seldom work with Shires full time. They need something tractable, not a test of skills every time the harness is put on.

Railway Horses

The term Gentle Giant is fondly if rather sentimentally used to describe the heavy horse. Those who worked with them for any length of time know that the term has no universal application. There are 'rogues' in all breeds, even though most of them are undoubtedly man-made.

One such was driven by Ernest Stocker on his first day at Moor Street Goods Station, Birmingham. The new driver knew none of this until he was pulling out of the yard, when a workmate warned him that the last driver was still in hospital after six months!

The warning was too late, for the horse had already set off, and continued unabated for two miles, when a long incline slowed him sufficiently to enable him to be turned round and headed back for town. There, a policeman on point duty saved the situation, and held the animal's head until Ernest Stocker could summon more help. But despite its faults, that horse could certainly pull.

A stable companion, Pansy, 'couldn't pull the skin off a rice pudding' – a horseman's favourite analogy. At the opposite end of the scale was Charlie, a big bay Shire driven by Andrew Mitchell from the London, Midland and Scottish depot in Coventry.

At the age of 78, Andrew Mitchell still recounted 'Charlie' anecdotes with relish:

He was standing in the main street while I was in a shop delivering. When I came out there was this posh Rolls Royce parked a few feet away. And there was this lady, with her chauffeur standing by watching, feeding Charlie from a big box of milk chocolates! About £4 or £5 worth, I reckon. He was a right softie, was Charlie. Although he had a sweet tooth he loved dandelions. I'd get on my bike early in the morning and ride out into the lanes and cut him a big faggot of dandelions.

Another railwayman, Ralph Matthews, was nicknamed 'Snatch' because he started on the railway as a chain horse boy. His job was to stand at the bottom of hills and steep inclines, hook his trace horse onto heavily laden rullies, and give them a 'snatch' up the hill.

Where association of ideas ends and intelligence begins is a debatable topic among animal students, but Dolly had more knowhow than most. Her driver, Ted Ward, used to send her on her own way after unhitching each evening, so that he could catch his train home (railway drivers did not feed their own horses).

I'd slap her flanks, click my tongue, 'Go on, now,' and she'd be away. She'd make her own way out of the station yard, up the street, into the bottom stable yard, across several sets of railway track, and into the top yard. There she'd go to her accustomed drinking trough, make her way past several stable blocks, walk past six or seven standings until she came to her own. She was almost human, that horse.

In 1936 the Great Western Railway began replacing horses with motor vehicles. But for the outbreak of war, this would have been completed in the early 1940s.

London, Midland and Scottish goods agent at Coventry, F.A. Caldwell, scorned the idea that his horse fleet should be completely disbanded. His words of warning have, over 40 years later, become a prophesy (see page 134): 'Horses – the faithful creatures – are far cheaper for short distance haulage work than mechanical horses and lorries . . . and their greater ability to manoeuvre means they are just as speedy.'

85

10 Wales and the Borders

The Montgomeryshire Society

Wales merits special mention in the story of Shire breeding. Scotland, the Isle of Man and Ireland prefer Clydesdales, though the Isle of Man Agricultural Society was among the list of Shire Horse Society members in 1914, but not in 1949.

At present Anglesey alone has seven Shire studs. The Shire classes at the Royal Welsh Show at Builth Wells are marvellous, but pride of place must go to the Welshpool Society, or the Montgomeryshire Entire Horse Society, as it is much better known.

The twice London Champion Vulcan (see page 30) was hired by the Society in 1892, together with Sir Albert Muntz's Dunsmore Forest King. The fee of £1,000 paid to Lord Ellesmere was the highest up to then, but results were not quite commensurate. J.R. Jones, commenting in about 1930 said: 'He [Vulcan] did not leave anything very great, but they were quite good sorts with the right class of legs, but most of his stock were on the small side.'

Vulcan was but one of a long line which established the Montgomeryshire Society at the top of the tree, an example to all stockbreeders of any class of stock anywhere in the world.

The bay Marshland Prince won at Welshpool in 1876, as a four-year-old, and was hired. His successor for the next two seasons was England's Wonder 761, who left several London Show winners. Many of his stock were strawberry roans like himself.

James Forshaw's King of Bucks 2815 was the 1884 choice. 'He left some big, weighty horse, and a great many were sold to go abroad. There was a great export trade just at that time; he was hired for £275,' Mr Jones tells us.

Two years later, the famous grey Lincolnshire Lad II was the Montgomeryshire stallion. His fee was £240, and at 14 years old he was 'as active as a four-year-old. He left a lot of grand animals, and was the means of giving Montgomeryshire a leg-up in the breeding of shires [sic] and undoubtedly was one of the best sires the breed has ever known'. He was hired again in 1888, and yet again in 1891, when he travelled the lower district.

Vulcan followed, and then Regent II 6316. He did so well that he was hired again in 1896 and 1897. Before this second hiring Bury Victor Chief was nominated; no one could say the Montgomeryshire Society was not ambitious. Yet Mr Jones comments that this great name 'did just fair'.

Buscot Harold and Markeaton Royal Harold were hired in 1902 and 1903 respectively, but unfortunately Mr Jones makes no comment on them. He praises Lockinge Albert: 'Several very good mares sired by this horse, and several foals sold at high prices.'

61 Welsh Judge Mr Llewellyn Joseph at the Bisquit Cognac Shire Horse of the Year Show at Wembley. Judging takes place outside in the afternoon, followed by an evening parade and presentation

Such a hiring system is an unparalleled proving ground for any sire: he is tested by the value and conformation of his offspring out of a wide variety of females living under a vast range of conditions. The hirings preceded the Milk Marketing Board's bull testing schemes by 80 years.

Another outstanding success among the Montgomeryshire Shires was Childwick Champion in 1907. He left a lot of very valuable animals in the county, and ranked with Lincolnshire Lad II and Carbon as doing very well for most members. But Birdsall Menestral was a disappointment (fig. 21). 'This horse did very badly, and it would have been a good thing for Montgomeryshire breeders if he had been shot before coming up,' says the redoubtable Mr Jones.

Childwick Champion was hired again in 1910–12, and the list thereafter reads like a Roll of Honour: Ratcliffe Forest King, Gaer Conqueror, Babingley Nulli Secundus, Theale Lockinge, Basildon Clansman and Moulton Harboro.

The Revival

The formation of the Abergele and District Shire Horse Society in February 1979 was a good indication of how the heavy horse has overcome the threat of extinction that faced it in the 1960s. The Editor of its newsletter writes:

Mechanization of transport and farming at one time threatened to push the heavy horses out of existence, but thanks to the few stalwarts who grimly battled against the iron monsters, the majestic giants of the heavy horse breeds – the Shires, Clydesdales, Suffolks and Percherons – are once again to be seen in great numbers at agricultural shows up and down the country. Many farmers use them for agricultural purposes and the breweries still use them for short-haul deliveries which they find more economical than motorized transport.

In 1920 there were over two million heavy horses in Britain, working on farms, canals, forests, pulling coal carts, railway waggons, brewers' drays, etc. By 1965 there were not more than 2,000 left. Then, the tide turned.

Was it the rising cost of fuel, the rising cost of maintenance of machinery or the soaring price of the machines themselves, or was there some other reason for this positive sign of the return of the heavy horse and a significant revival of interest in them?

We can only guess at the reason, but one thing is certain, the heavy horse is back. There is evidence of this in the number of horses shown at the Spring Shows in Peterborough, the ever-increasing number of Shires and other heavy horses shown in local shows and the growing interest shown by the public in these magnificent animals.

The Elian Shires

Bryn Elian Farm, Dolwen, near Abergele has been connected with Shires for nearly 200 years. J.D.P. Williams, the present Shire breeder, is the sixth generation of the family to breed Shires there. The most notable member of the family in the Shire world was Mr Williams's grandfather on his mother's side, the late J.K. Jones, who died suddenly at the age of 75 as a result of a tragic accident on the farm in February 1955. Following his death, the farm passed to his daughter and son-in-law who are still resident at Bryn Elian.

At the time of Mr Jones' death, there were four Shires on the farm, and it was decided that they should be sold, but fortunately, due to the influence of Mr W.H. Hughes, the groom at Bryn Elian, Mrs Williams was persuaded to keep one of the horses, namely Elian Flower, a mare foaled in 1953 who was to remain at Bryn Elian for 23 years. Elian Flower was shown at a number of local shows from the age of two years and gained many prizes.

During this time, Derrick Williams, who had started working with a firm of auctioneers, was taking more and more interest in the farm and the horses in particular. It was in 1961 at the age of 18 that he took Elian Flower to the noted stallion Alneland Delegate, standing at Sarn in Anglesey, and as a result the mare gave birth to a bay colt foal in May 1962. This was the year that Mr J.D.P. Williams came into the Shire world. He took Elian Flower with her colt, Elian Winston, to the North Wales Show at Caernarvon where he won first prize in the brood mare class and second with her foal. During the rest of the 1962 season, the mare and foal were shown at most of the shows in north Wales and ended the season by winning first prize with the mare and foal at the Cerrigydrudion Show.

In 1967, Elian Flower gave birth to a black filly foal by Grangewood Bengie, the foal being registered as Elian Fair Lady who is still at Bryn Elian and has had eight foals.

In 1968, Mr Williams bought a nine-year-old 18-hands-high dapple grey mare, Park Grey Queen, from John Suckley for £155. After only three weeks the horse was sold to the United States.

In 1970, Derrick Williams purchased a mare and colt foal from G. Lloyd Owen, Anglesey. The mare was Culcliffe Susan Diane. The colt was not shown until he was two years old when he won first prize in the gelding class at the Royal Lancashire Show in Blackpool. This success was followed a few weeks later by a first prize at the Montgomery Show, but he was sold at the showground to Arthur Wright Farms Ltd. He went on to win prizes at most of the major shows up and down the country and in 1976 he won the supreme champion award in the gelding class at the Shire Horse Society Spring Show in Peterborough.

In the meantime Culcliffe Susan Diane foaled a grey colt in 1973, Elian Grey King, which was to become famous as a stallion at John Suckley's Alneland Stud. He won in his class three times in succession as a yearling, a two-year-old and as a three-year-old.

In 1973 and 1979, Derrick Williams won the championship foal cup in the Oswestry Show.

In 1976, a yearling filly, Elian Lady Grey, was sold to A. and F. Weintraub, Big Foot Ranch, California, and in 1979 she was grand champion at the California State Fair and National Shire Show.

In 1978, Elian Grey Queen, foaled by Elian Fair Lady and sired by Elian Grey King won first prize at the Denbigh and Flint Show as well as being reserve supreme champion, female champion and county champion. The same year, she won first prize and the prize for champion yearling at the Liverpool Show, gained a first at Eglwysbach and was reserve champion at Cerrigydrudion.

In 1979, she was second as a two-year-old at Oswestry, second at Denbigh and Flint as well as reserve female champion and county champion. At the same show, she was junior champion for three-year-olds and under as well as reserve supreme champion for the Parkington Golden Guinea Award.

This is a very brief story of the Elian Shires. In the future we look forward to hearing of more successes. At the time of writing there are two mares, two three-year-old fillies and two colt foals at Bryn Elian.

On show in the farmhouse is the evidence of Shire breeding success. Pictures of prize-winning Shires, and rosettes, mostly red in colour, denoting first prizes, are hanging on the walls and stored in drawers and in chests. A couple of old albums of photographs bring back nostalgic memories of days gone by.

Walking in the Furrow

This is a story of a man who spent most of his working life with horses, a man who would plough an acre a day – a man who walked in the furrow. William Henry Hughes of Bryn Elian, Colwyn Bay, was born at Tan Dderwen, Llanelian in the days when horses on the roads and farms were simply taken for granted.

At the age of 14 William Hughes left school to become a farm hand at Ty Hwnt i'r Afon and during his first year he was employed as a general help on the farm, tending sheep and cattle. There were at that time two teams of Shires on the farm and two men to work them. During the second year the second teamsman became ill and at the age of 15 William Hughes was asked to take charge of the team. At that time there were some 80 acres of land under plough.

At the end of his third year he moved to Bryn Elian where Mr J.K. Jones took him on as teamsman and it was here he was to spend most of his working life. Mr J.K. Jones, grandfather of J.D.P. Williams, was always referred to as 'the gaffer'.

When Mr Hughes started at Bryn Elian there were two working teams of Shires on the farm, and another team known as the 'show team' in the stables as well as another dozen or so colts, geldings and mares roaming the fields. This was the time when coal, fertilizers and feedstuffs had to be hauled from the depot in town and Mr Hughes remembers these journeys well, particularly when the gaffer used to meet him half way home with an unbroken horse which would be hitched in line between the team to haul the load up the hill towards Bryn Elian. As soon as the load was in the yard the unbroken horse would be hitched to a chain harrow for an hour or two. It was always the gaffer who would be in charge of the breaking-in of young horses. Mr Hughes says there was no performance about breaking-in in those days; it just came naturally. He also remembers one of the mares in his first-ever team at Bryn Elian, who always thought the grass was greener on the other side of the hedge and was continually breaking through to other fields. She was sold as a five-year-old.

At this time at Bryn Elian there would be about 60 acres of hay to be harvested, and during the harvest it would be all hands on deck. There would be the gaffer, the cowman and his assistant as well as the two teamsters, and two casual workers taken on for the harvest season.

Mr Hughes and the other three hands slept in the stable lofts, and at 5 o'clock every morning the gaffer would knock the ceiling of the stable below with his stick to wake the men. During the harvest time if the weather was good, the stick would wake them at 4 a.m. They would then cut hay until about 9 a.m., after which they would start carrying hay that was ready for stacking and would be at it sometimes until 10 o'clock at night.

Normally all the hands would help to milk the 35 or so milking cows in order that the milk could be taken to town to be in the dairy by 7 a.m. During the harvest the teamsters would be excused this task.

So the years rolled by and Mr Hughes and his horses toiled away. Apart from the harvest there would be the ploughing, the planting, seeding and gathering of the root crops such as potatoes, swedes etc., and the never ending supply of manure from the stables and cowshed, which had to be taken to the fields. There was also the annual threshing when all the farms in the area would help each other. This entailed hauling the heavy threshing machine and its steam boiler from farm to farm, and often this would be done at a late hour so that the 'engineers', as they were called, could start the threshing early the following day.

One of Mr Hughes' pet subjects is ploughing, and on listening to him one can tell that he is an expert on the subject. He is reluctant to boast about his achievements but he revealed that on the third Wednesday of November 1939 he started to plough an area of 25 acres and he had completed it all before the Christmas break – an average of just over an acre a day. His ploughing day would be from 8.30 a.m. when he left the yard at Bryn Elian to walk the half-hour journey to the field, until he arrived back at the yard at 4.30 p.m. He well remembers the day he started because it was the day of the annual fair at Abergele. At that time at Bryn Elian there were 53 acres under plough and he would plough it all himself.

The competitive ploughing bug bit William Hughes when he was in his first year at Bryn Elian. It was the gaffer, J.K. Jones, who asked him if he would plough with the Bryn Elian team in the ploughing match to be held at Betws yn Rhos. He was only 17 at the time, and he won third prize in his class and the judges told him that his furrow horse, instead of walking in the furrow, had walked on the furrow slice turned over on the previous time round. This was something the ploughman could do nothing about except to change over the furrow horse with the land horse. This was Mr Hughes' first ploughing match and he says it got hold of him. He can remember the first ploughing match at Llanelian which took place in 1928.

For the first two or three years he did not win anything higher than a third prize, until he was able to borrow a prize plough from the Wrexham area with which he won first prize at Betws yn Rhos in the under-30s class. Two weeks later he won first prize in a class of ten top ploughmen and the prize was £10 from which he had to pay £2 for the loan of the team. From this time on he won many prizes and he has the distinction of owning the championship cup awarded at the last ploughing match to be held at Betws yn Rhos. It was at Rhuddlan ploughing match that he saw the first tractor ploughing, and it was here also that he swept the board, winning first prizes for the 'scratch', the 'ridge', the 'trim' and the 'crown' as well as the cup for champion ploughman.

The trophies on display at Bryn Elian are the results of his many achievements behind the plough, and a constant reminder to William Hughes of the days he walked in the furrow.

Alneland Dispersal

On 19 September 1981, one of the most important sales during the heavy horse's revival period took place. John Suckley was obliged through ill health to disperse the Alneland Stud which he had built up over the preceding years.

Eaton & Hollis, the Derby auctioneers, claimed this stud with its 42 horses to be the largest in the British Isles. Other Shire studs may have had more mares, yet the Alneland Stud was renowned for the choice and number of its stallions, and Mr Suckley certainly hired out more stallions than any other Shire breeder.

The Alneland stud was housed a mile from Oswestry, Shropshire, and on

that September morning an unceasing procession of cars passed through its yard for the car park. A crowd estimated at 3,000 assembled; 90 percent of them were dedicated Shire people. The balance were interested amateurs, taking advantage of the occasion to add to their photographs or sound recordings.

The sale was a reminder of life in the earlier horse era, when a score of horses would be sold at any large farm dispersal. Young horses filled one six-stall stable; others were haltered around a capacious fold yard, while the loose boxes housed an assortment of stallions, and mares and foals.

The brief catalogued pedigrees read like a manual of Shires. Dunderdales Rose, Elton Lad, Crossfield Supreme, Edingdale Marina 2nd, Alneland Masterpiece II, Bellasize Elizabeth, Hainton Explorer, Blankney Marina – they all represent some of the very top blood in the breed.

Among the two-year-old colts was Ladbrook Harvester, by Arthur Lewis's favourite stallion Bulbridge Traveller (see page 118) out of Fenns Wood Primrose. He made 475 guineas.

Woodhouse Footprint, Whiteley Winston and Quixhill Masterpiece

Top left
62   Knowing eyes scrutinize a Shire at the Alneland sale

Bottom left
63   The Shire's revival has never been better demonstrated than by the massed crowds at the Alneland stud dispersal sale, at Brogyntyn Farm, Oswestry, Shropshire, in autumn 1981

Above
64   A pile of shoes that once fitted Mr John Suckley's Alneland Shires

figure in the mares' pedigrees, and Far Barsey Princess had a colt foal by the notable Shire Edingale Mascot. Princess was dark bay/roan, 13 years old and made 1,000 guineas.

It is always interesting to note cross-bred produce from Shires. Alneland Variety had produced a 160-guineas dark bay colt foal by the Hackney stallion Manorside John, while a Cob × Hackney mare was in foal again to the same stallion. The foal by her side was by Ryefield Select. Like some other excellent offspring, this one was unplanned, for the dam was a rather wild and seldom handled mare that broke through to the Shire stallion when in season, and a grand dark-coloured, short-coupled colt foal resulted. The mare realized 500 guineas, the foal 210 guineas.

Ty Fry Mistress sold well among the fillies. Her sire was Skelton Masterpiece, and the dam Ty Fry Beauty and their bay/black offspring sold for 620 guineas.

Although a sense of personal sadness is inevitable when any great breeder retires, the sale was much less of a catastrophe than if it had been held 20 years earlier. Then, 90 per cent of the horses would have gone to the butcher which would have broken John Suckley's heart. Though a local butcher did take away a few animals, the bulk at the 1981 event went to fellow breeders and exhibitors.

Thus the stock found many new homes and infiltrated the Shire world in a way that can only be beneficial. There were greys to breed yet more greys – Mr Suckley was always a great protagonist of the colour. The top-selling greys were the two-year-old Gilda Diamond Queen at 1,650 guineas; the three-year-old Charnes Boadicea, 835 guineas; and the two-year-old colt Elian Grey Prince at 660 guineas. Other splendid stallions fit to fill the needs of hiring societies and private breeders were sold.

One such breeder was Mr Coates of Kent, who bought Alneland Masterpiece II, a stallion which had gone fairly pale with age, and realized 650 guineas.

Pick of the stallions was the black Ryefield Select, also eight years old, and by Lymm Advance out of Ryefield Pat. He sold for 2,700 guineas and was hired to the Montgomeryshire Society, for years in the forefront of Shire breeding (see page 86).

11 The Shire in North America

When North America was first settled by white men, the power they used consisted of their own muscle and the wiry ponies already there. Ox teams also played their part. Massive importations of heavy draught stallions did not begin until the late nineteenth century. The first importation of ten Shires was made in 1880, but by 1887 the number had risen to 339. The first volume of the *American Shire Horse Association Stud Book* was published in 1888, and lists 935 stallions and 246 mares.

Importing stallions had quickly become big business. Of that 1,181 total, only 132 were home bred. The instigators of the *Stud Book* were also importers, and used the book as a selling aid as well as a tool for breeders.

The reasons for the demand for heavy horses are easily traced. In several

65 Here is the old type of Shire of the 1920s or '30s. He is an unidentified stallion standing in North America, and as such is guaranteed to add bone and weight substance to the offspring of any cross-bred mare that happens to make up the teams. The settlers wanted something to pull and to breed pullers, without too much finesse

states, homesteads of 160 acres were being mapped out. Such blocks measured on average half a mile each way, and were named quarter sections. A section was a square mile or 640 acres. Advertisements appeared in Britain offering cheap travel to reach them. So, naturally, British horses were called for.

Serving these new farmers was a flight of machinery makers. Demand led to prosperity and enterprise. One new design succeeded the last and, just as in today's tractor industry, the latest models were bigger and heavier than their precedents. So they needed more and stronger horses to pull them.

Cities linked by railways were also growing. The goods piled by the rail sidings had to be moved to warehouses, then to the retailer, and finally to the consumer. Each activity called for power, and the scarcity of labour induced big horses and big teams in which to drive them.

Chicago, in the heart of the corn belt, was the centre of all this activity. The Union Stock Yards were fashioned, and led to the International Livestock Show. Most American stud books, flock books and herd books originated in Chicago hotels during this period, and those who know the Shire men of today will have no difficulty in imagining the late night discussions and the liberal oiling with barley products that surrounded the birth of these exciting new ventures!

Pedigree became important. Illinois and, to a lesser extent, Iowa, were the importers' bases, and led to the establishment of many farmer-breeders in those two states.

Livestock breed societies have generally been extremely fortunate in the calibre of their staff. Charles Burgess of Wenona was the American Shire Horse Association's first secretary, a post he carried for 30 years. John Truman of Bushnell, Illinois, became president in 1902, continued for 22 years, and later became secretary. Both were large scale importers, as were the Finch brothers from Verona, and Joliet and Taylor Jones from Williamsville.

The import business really boomed during the 1880s. Then farming slumped in the '90s, and many fewer stallions were brought in. Although stud books were published in 1888, 1890 and 1892, Volume 4 did not meet the printer's ink until 1900. In this volume American-bred Shires were in the majority for the first time, numbering 1,067 of the 1,432 horses registered.

Stallion registrations continued to outstrip the mares', with 861 against 571. In those busy days, farmers were more concerned with upgrading their lighter-legged stock than with establishing pure-bred studs. They needed animals to make up the big teams and pull the big implements, and these animals were provided by Shire stallions and those of other draught breeds, out of cross-bred mares.

To cope with the demand for draught stallions, few importers stuck to one breed. Even such Shire people as George Brown of Aurora and the Truman family dealt in other breeds, although never masking where their preference lay. Men who became famous in other breeds also dealt in Shires. They included the father of the American Percheron breed, Mark Dunham, besides A.B. Holbert and Singmasters from Iowa, and the Bell Brothers from Ohio.

The turn of the century was also a turning point in the heavy-horse world. Although it had taken eight years up to 1900 to produce Volume 4 of the *American Shire Horse Association Stud Book*, Volume 5 arrived in 1904. It contained 1,850 pedigrees, over 700 being imported horses. The total

number of horses registered in these four years was a third more than in the preceding eight.

The years 1904–14 were fondly regarded as the best by many who lived through them, and with regret by those who missed them. In the Shire world, there is ample reason for such nostalgia. All the draught breeds were expanding rapidly. Volumes 6 to 9 of the *Stud Book* were issued, one every two or three years, and covered the most active decade in the breed's history.

Of 7,227 registrations, American-bred Shires accounted for 4,271, imports for 2,956. Some 300 Shires left England for America every year during the period.

66 Though it is possible to pick out specimens of other breeds, Shires predominate in this Blackfoot Fair scene. Decorated straps are a feature of American harness. Some are purely for show, whereas most British decorations are attached to functional leather. The judge was Alma Chaffin

Bell Brothers, Dunhams, Holberts and Singmasters concentrated their main attention on other breeds and dealt less in the Shire. Others took their place. A.C. Ruby of Portland, Ohio, Peter Hopley & Sons from Lewis, Ohio, and Henry Wheatley of California began to operate on a large scale.

The peak of Shire importations was reached in 1910 and 1911. We must thank Arlin Wareing, Blackfoot, Idaho (an importer today, who helped spark off the British revival) for counting the Truman family's imports. In 1910 they brought over 200 out of 466, and in the following year 105 out of 504.

During the years 1900–17, 3,907 Shires migrated to the United States. Of these, 1,032, or over a quarter, passed through the Trumans' hands. The family both bought and bred grey Shires, and the Americans, used to the grey Percheron, regarded them highly.

The total horse population in the United States at the turn of the century was 13,537,000 and still growing. According to one American writer, at least half of them contained 'from ten to 50 per cent Great War Horse blood'. So if more weight was wanted, there was an ample basis on which to build.

A farmer writing from the North-West Territory of Canada in 1905 said:

The only thing in the stock line that there is much money in is horses; they are keeping high, and seem likely to for years, as so many new settlers are coming in all the time, and others do not seem able to raise enough for their own needs; and it may be mentioned that almost the only kind of stallions available there are of the Percheron breed, which is certainly not calculated to improve the size, or substance, of the native draught horse stock.

Will Percheron friends please note that this is a quote!

The *Farmer and Stockbreeder Year Book* is an invaluable periodical for all interested in heavy horses. The real value of horseflesh as part of the tenant farmer's economy is highlighted time and again. In its early days, pedigree Shire breeding was largely in the admittedly enthusiastic and capable hands of the more prosperous nobility, landowners and farmers, but as the twentieth century progressed the benefits of Shire breeding spread more widely.

In 1906 S.H.L. (J.A. Frost) wrote in the *Year Book*:

The Old English breed of cart horse, or 'Shire', is universally admitted to be the best and most valuable animal for draught purposes in the world, and a visitor from America, Mr Morrow, of the United States Department of Agriculture, speaking at Mr John Rowell's sale of Shires in 1889, said, 'Great as had been the business done in Shire horses in America, the trade is but in its infancy, for the more Shire horses became known, and the more they came into competition with other breeds, the more their merits for all heavy draught purposes were appreciated'.

These remarks are true to-day [1906], for although sixteen years have elapsed since they were made, the massive Shire has more than held his own, but in the interests of the breed, and of the nearly four thousand members of the Shire Horse Society, it is still doubtful whether the true worth of the Shire horse is properly known and appreciated in foreign countries and towns needing heavy horses, and whether the export trade in this essentially British breed is not capable of further development. The number of export certificates granted by the Shire Horse Society in 1889 was 1264, which takes a good deal of beating, but it must be remembered that since then Shire horse breeding at home has progressed by leaps and bounds, and tenant farmers, who could only look on in those days, are now members of the flourishing Shire Horse Society and owners of breeding studs, and such prices as 800 guineas for a two-year-old filly and

230 guineas for a nine-month-old colt, are less frequently obtainable than they were then; therefore, an increase in the demand from other countries would find more Shire breeders ready to supply it, although up to the present the home demand has been and is very good, and weighty geldings continue to be scarce and dear.

The horse business, and especially the stallion importing business, had been very good in America for a few years. With so many people jumping onto the importing bandwaggon, there was a danger of overdoing it. For this reason the major importers were asked for their views. Almost unanimously, they made three points:

1 That while their own business was steady, they felt that the country was beginning to be adequately stocked with stallions.

2 The intense demand for pure-bred mares still did not persuade farmers to pay sufficient to make widespread importations profitable.

3 Top quality heavy draught geldings formed the top of the market, but the number of quality mares to breed them was lacking.

67 The Mackay Rodeo Parade, Idaho. The high-sided four-wheeled vehicle has been a popular design in North America since horses became widespread

British Strains in America

The Evans family had much to do with early Shire history in Iowa. In the decade before World War One, George Evans and W.A. Evans, both from Eagle Grove, were buying Shire mares from Bill Crownover and Frank Huddlestun.

In the '30s Harvey Evans dealt in Belgians and bred Percherons from the same address. Before then, he was a Shire man. In 1919 he bought a very good nine-year-old registered Shire mare from George Evans named Boro' Vanity.

A chapter in Keith Chivers's *The Shire Horse* is headed 'They All Go Back to Harold'. In it he describes how the great foundation horse might easily have been shipped to America before he was proven. In fact his genes crossed the ocean many times, and Boro' Vanity has Harold on both sides of her pedigree.

Boro' Vanity's breeder was Mrs Salt, from Belper, Derbyshire – still a famous name in Shire circles. The mare's sire, Offley Harold 21730, was a bay with a blaze and four white legs, as was his sire Bury Premier Duke 16575. And *his* sire was Harold 3703.

Harold, foaled 1881, was brown with white face and hind legs. The 1885 *Stud Book* allocates him seven lines. But the very entry catches the heartstrings of a present-day Shire lover. For with Harold's sire, the grey Lincolnshire Lad II 1365 and his dam's sire Champion 419, we are back in Volume I of the *Stud Book* and the dawn of worthwhile Shire history.

Boro' Vanity's dam was Rose 43142 by Hendre Hercules 17386, whose sire Prince Harold 14228 was by Harold. On this pleasant genealogical trip we find that Prince Harold, foaled 1890, won at Wirral and Birkenhead as a foal, while in the next two years he headed eight leading shows, from Ormskirk and Southport through the second Yorkshire Show at Middlesbrough, and including Peterborough and the Suffolk Show at Bury St Edmunds.

Severn Flag, Huddlestun's chief stock horse, was used with lasting success on Boro' Vanity. Two of her foals, Boro' Buster and Boro' Flag, were both noted winners, the latter being sold to Huddlestun in 1923. Boro' Flag won his class at Chicago four times, and with his brother won the Produce of Dam class at Chicago in 1924.

During the 1920s, Evans's best show mare was Ashdale Bonnie, by Severn Flag out of Boro' Lady. Purchases included the bay Quality May in 1921, and the sorrel Pansy in 1924. Boro' Buster was the horse used on these three, and their progeny makes up much of the Evans story in Shires.

Another breeder who benefited through proximity to Huddlestun's stallions was John Butler, Webster City. For Frank Huddlestun was to Shires in Iowa what John Truman was to them in Illinois. They were president and secretary respectively of the American breed society during the 1930s, but they did not get on. Truman remained loyal to the English stamp of Shire ('wooden legs', his horses were termed by their critics); Huddlestun tried to please the American farmer with cleaner-legged animals.

Iowa found in Frank Huddlestun a voice and leader in draught-horse matters. For many years he was president of the Iowa Horse and Mule Breeders' Association, and his first known purchase of registered Shires was in 1905 when he bought Newton Ringlet and Vera of Glendale. The latter bred filly foals in 1905 and 1906, Vera of Edgewood and Belle of the Farm.

In 1918 Ralph Fogleman bought these two as foundation mares for his new stable.

Diverging views did not stop Truman and Huddlestun from trading with each other, and being outstanding breeders they both benefited.

Severn Flag was bought in 1918 after winning the championship of the 1913 Illinois State Fair. He replaced Bury Cannon Ball, a bay imported by Truman and bought by Huddlestun in 1914.

In all, Huddlestun bred over 130 registered Shires, far more than anyone else in Iowa. He bought and sold many more. Some 20 mares were bought during the stable's foundation, the queen mother of the lot proving to be Heale Easter Eve, a brown imported mare.

Heale Easter Eve was a brown with white face and three white legs, the near foreleg being black. She was owned by the Hon. Louis Greville, Heale House, Woodford, Salisbury, and was got by the famous Blythwood Conqueror, 14997. That horse's sire was Hitchin Conqueror, and his grandsire William the Conqueror.

In 1939, Frank Huddlestun died. His Edgewood Farm on Webster City's outskirts was noted for being a model of neatness, with everything in its place. His stock carried on much longer. The pedigrees of the 1941 Chicago Show winners were:

Royal Lee
Grand champion stallion
shown by Fox Chemical Co., Des Moines, Iowa

Lee Ander
Huddlestun-bred

Royal William Jr
Huddlestun's last major herd sire, Des Moines champion

Olena
A Huddlestun-bred Chicago and Des Moines grand champion by Tatton Dray King II

September Morn
Huddlestun-bred

Tatton Dray King II
Huddlestun herd sire during the '20s, Des Moines champion

Mildred C
Huddlestun-bred daughter of Severn Flag, grand champion Chicago, 1925

Lady Jean
Grand champion mare,
shown by Geo. J. Stoll
& Sons, Chestnut, Illinois

Prince
Schaffenacker-bred

Edgewood Zella
Grand champion mare,
Chicago 1936, Huddlestun-bred

Royal William Jr
See above

Ethlene
Huddlestun-bred daughter of Severn Flag and one of his greatest brood mares

Decline and Rise in America

Though the Shire made up only a small proportion of the North American draught-horse population, it was still of considerable importance in view of the vast total draught-horse numbers. The Percheron scored through its adaptability as a road horse in the early days, better able to work in the fields and then be driven to a buggy at weekends.

After World War One, the Belgian became second numerically. Its phlegmatic disposition and slow speed made it suitable for the changing and possibly unskilled men moving about the countryside. Clyde and Shire came next, and Suffolks last.

From the start, the Mid-West was the heartland of farming, and the centre of the draught-horse industry. It had areas of heavy land which did not suit the Shires' feathery legs, but most of the large breeders had their studs there. It was also handy for the promotional areas of Chicago, Ohio and Indiana.

In the Far West, the farms were bigger, but there was less tillage and a lighter soil. To tie in what is happening today, it is necessary to realise this background, for the two large areas had different types of Shire, with a Far West, Mid-West and now an English type of Shire each having its firm and vocal adherents. Arlin Wareing has tried hard to unify the fragments, and

68 Alma Chaffin with two Shires in splendid condition. Had this comparatively clean-legged type of Shire been available in the late nineteenth century, the breed might have been still more popular in America

confesses failure to date. But the types of American Shire are still combined in one stud book.

'Today's English Shire is not as hard to handle as our native Shires,' he said; 'This may be because in the Far West so many lighter animals were used to cross with the Shire, and the spirit came from them.'

Tractors first came to the Mid-West before World War Two, but there were still as many horses about, though fewer registrations. Then some of the big breeders started to sell, as tractors took more and more of the market.

One of the buyers was Fred H. Bixby of Long Beach, California. An oil multi-millionaire, he made draught horses his hobby. He chose his own type of Shire – not too big, but suited to all-round use. He had both funds and facilities, including three main ranches and some others. At one time he was reputed to own 500 Shire horses.

This operation continued until Fred Bixby died in the early 1950s. Meanwhile, after World War Two, the tractors took over, and draught horses disappeared virtually overnight.

Life-long horse dealer Alma Chaffin was born in the nineteenth century. He was but one of many concerned in the slaughter trade, for there was no other outlet. In one year alone he sold 1,500 draught horses to slaughter houses, where they became dog meat.

One of the few men to keep their horses was C.J. Wright, in the Snake River Valley, Idaho. In 1948 he visited California to see Bixby's horses, and returned with 16 head. These were mainly to compete at the East Idaho State Fair and other shows throughout the year, where the six-horse hitch was the ultimate in showmanship. Being of the Bixby type, these 16 horses set the standard at Idaho, for there were few others.

After Fred Bixby's death, his daughter Elizabeth Janeway was alone among his heirs in trying to preserve his horses and ideals. This was to be his memorial. But she was not really a horsewoman, and did not even know the name of the Idaho buyer, C.J. Wright, who might have some remaining stock.

During her searches in 1952 she met Vernon Bird and, through him, Alma Chaffin. This set them in mind to buy Shires again, Vernon Bird for a show hitch and Alma Chaffin to make money, but also because he liked the big horses best. They visited the Bixby California ranch, bought the show hitch of blacks with white markings, and some for Alma Chaffin. The latter thereupon bid a lower price for taking the next ten, and still lower one for a further ten. They ended up with 33 head at an average price of $75 each including three stallions, and returned with them to Idaho. These horses saved the American Shire from extinction, for Alma Chaffin sold them throughout the inter-mountain West at $125 each.

Meanwhile Mrs Janeway established her eight- or ten-horse hitch, and in the mid-1970s Arlin Wareing saw four of them still alive and fit, at over 30 years of age! They had of course lived their lives in near ideal conditions.

On the death of Bixby, the American Shire Horse Association had virtually ceased to function. Registrations dwindled. Then an extraordinary thing occurred. The then secretary determined to write a book entitled *The Rise and Fall of the Shire Horse*. He could not use this title if Shire registrations continued, so he refused to accept any. Records ceased in 1953.

This seemed the end. But strange things happen in livestock breeding, and the third remaining Shire stallion was found on a farm, the first having gone to Nevada where all efforts to trace him or any descendants failed. The second was with Vernon Bird.

The owner of stallion number three had his hip crushed by another horse, and determined to sell his stud. Donald Anderson from Washington saw the advertisement, and travelled a thousand miles to see and buy the stallion.

When he took the horse home, he found he couldn't register it. He had paid a pedigree price for an animal that could not be transferred in the stud book, because no stud book existed. He sought the help of Edwin Hinken, a young civil engineer (now a Clydesdale breeder) who proceeded to spend a great deal of his own time and money in piecing together the Shire register, for which he has never had the credit he deserves. He did the same for the Suffolks. Later he contacted Lester Good, a leading Belgian breeder in Illinois. Together they traced books and papers located in the late secretary's shed, whose death had occurred in the intervening years.

Vernon Bird was a leading breeder and a great horseman, but he did not enjoy paper work. It was not easy to persuade him to set down his knowledge of pedigrees and back-breeding, but Ed Hinken forced him into it.

Don Anderson's stallion could not perpetuate the line, and left very few offspring. So from the Bixby-bred 33 in 1953, the Shire breed lost still further ground until in 1965–6 there were only 25 registered Shire horses in the whole of America.

It would have been difficult enough to breed up from so small a nucleus even if the stock had been unrelated. They were not. Fred Bixby had carried out a careful programme of line- and in-breeding, so that these few existing Shires were all of one blood line. Infertility troubles were followed by poor viability if a full-term foal was born, and by abnormalities.

In 1964, only two Shire foals were born in the whole of America. In that year Maurice Telleen started a little magazine, *Draft Horse Journal*, which became the link between all breeders and all breeds of heavy horse.

In 1966, Arlin Wareing became actively involved, and found the situation so desperate that he decided to find what the Motherland had to offer. So he visited England in 1966–7, and bought Jim's Chieftain, a yearling colt from the old-established stud of Mr Jim Cooke.

Jim's Chieftain was used as a two-year-old, when he left three foals. In the next season he left eight, from virtually all the available Shire mares in the USA. 'Without the importation of Jim's Chieftain, the Shire horse would have been lost to us,' Arlin Wareing remarked.

Two further importations followed. Ladbrook Jock arrived in 1968, followed by the mare Bellasize Charm II in 1969. Having assessed the potential, Arlin Wareing met Maurice Telleen at a Mid-West show, and together they arranged and co-hosted a trip to England, Wales and Scotland in 1970.

A merry party of 45 Canadian and American horsemen arrived, had the time of their lives, and departed with eight horses. Since then 100 head have crossed the Atlantic, half bought by Arlin Wareing, who assisted with some of the others.

These English bloodlines have taken over the breed in America, but not without furore. Adherents of the Bixby type won't admit that these imports are true Shires. The importers believe that the usual 16.2 hands height of the Bixby type is insufficient for today's market. The Belgians, Budweisser Clydesdales and Percherons are all much taller.

'Though English Shires may possibly have lost a little substance, they are considerably better than they were ten years ago,' claimed Arlin Wareing.

In 1980 the American register was composed of 147 registered Shire females, 91 stallions and 127 grading-up mares. This is an improvement of

1,000 per cent on the low of 1965–6.

Black with four white legs and a white blaze, a ton weight and 18 hands high is the favoured USA combination.

One major technical disappointment has affected the far-flung countrysides of America and Australia. Embryo transfer, which has had some success in light horses, has proved a dismal failure among heavies. Of ten transfers at the Colorado Veterinary School, it is doubtful if one had succeeded at the last report.

The technique, well established in the cattle world, involves fertilization of the ova, followed by collection of the embryo, and its implantation in a carrier mare. In theory, a brood mare could supply an embryo foal at every heat period, perhaps five or six a year, which would be carried to birth by mares of any breed.

Though the Shire Horse Society has accepted embryo transfer, much more work obviously is needed before the technique makes an impact on the heavy-horse world.

Work on an American Farm

Winters are tough indeed at Moran, Wyoming, near the Yellowstone National Park. Here Walt Feuz (pronounced 'fates') and his wife Betty have run a family ranch for many years, and relied on horses for most of their power.

The horses haul fodder to a herd of 400 Hereford cows and, though a medium-sized Fordson tractor has been purchased, it is far less essential than the Shires.

In the low temperatures endured every winter, the horses have one great

69 Winter in Blackfoot. Horses retained their place on American farms and ranches to a far greater extent than was generally the case in Britain. The teams have cold weather advantages in regions where the thermometer really sinks and batteries may fail

advantage. They work. Batteries and fuel pipes don't. And when the snow drifts are deepest, a bobsleigh powered by a four-Shire team ensures that the cattle do not go hungry.

The wheel horses are greys, Mike and Pat. The lead pair are bays, Mack and Turk. When pulling hay, the leaders are unyoked and hitched to the pole tripod by a cable. A grapple fork is pushed, prong by prong, into the loose hay. The team pulls away and the hay swings into the air and over the hayrack. The release cord is pulled on a signal from the person in the rack, dropping the hay into place. The process is repeated until the rack is filled.

Sleigh runners sometimes freeze in place as spring approaches and melting snow leaves pools of water around them. Overnight frost requires a fair pull to free the sledge, but Mike and Pat are equal to the call. Winter feeding seldom takes more than half a day, when the men return for a big meal and the horses to their warm log barn.

This winter routine means that the Shires are worked hard for only six months of the year. They last around 23 years under such conditions, and even then are self-replacing. Walt Feuz kept two Shire mares, Bird and Kate, as breeders. Recently both foaled on the same day, but sadly Kate died giving birth. Her companion accepted the orphan, and reared both foals without trouble.

Both mares were big, upstanding animals, of lighter colour than is fashionable in Britain, but of a weight that would remind breeders there of 'the good old-fashioned sort'. Work starts with the three-year-olds.

Montana rancher/writer Spike Van Cleve captured the horseman's spirit and relationship with his animals in a short story *Cody and Terry*. Working horses give rise to such yarns, tractors never.

Years passed, and the two got pretty grey around the heads, but whatever they were asked to do they still did in a workmanlike fashion. There were younger teams for the hard work, and finally we only used them for getting out a little timber in the winter, mainly really so we'd have an excuse to see that they had plenty of grain in the rough weather. This was right down Cody's alley, since it was all light downhill work, but that didn't keep the smart son of a gun from taking Terry and slipping off to the barn with him any time they were left alone in the timber. A man automatically took a hitch around the nearest stump with the log chain before dropping them. You could watch Cody stealthily test out the hitch first one way and then the other to see if it was solid.

12 The Big Teams

'Practice with Science' is the motto of the Royal Agricultural Society of England, but nowhere has it been better applied than on the vast ploughlands of North America. Professors of the United States universities were working in conjunction with teamsters at a time when much deeper gulfs separated farm workers and scientists in Britain.

Intensive study in the colleges was applied quickly to the land, and the burden of the teachings would be acceptable to any stockman. 'Good farmers try to treat their horses as they would wish to be treated themselves if they were work animals instead of men' is an admirable precept whether it comes from Church or college.

Correctly designed, properly adjusted hitches permit animals to exert their strength most advantageously and allow the use of enough animals to supply ample power. When horses are driven and hitched to the multi-hitches, and properly adjusted sharp implements are used, output should be on the following scale:

1 The four-horse team will plough four acres a day, single disc 20 acres, or harrow 40 acres.

2 The five-horse team will plough five acres a day, single disc 25 acres, or harrow 50 acres.

3 The six-horse team will plough six acres a day, single disc 30 acres, or harrow 60 acres.

4 The eight-horse team will plough eight acres a day, single disc 40 acres, and harrow 80 acres.

And so on.

The Horse and Mule Association of America was instrumental in bringing physics and mathematics to the dust cloud of the big team. It answered many practical questions.

Teams are strung out in tandem fashion to make a more compact team for handling, and to bring the true line of pull of the team over the true line of draught of ploughs or binders. Important ancillary aims are the elimination of side draught, overheating, crowding, and abuse of the animals. The Shires and Shire-crosses cannot give of their best if they are bundled tightly together on a hot day.

On discs, harrows and drills the teams may be hitched abreast, as all horses are walking over the same type of cultivated ground, and there is no side draught to contend with. Even so, it is more convenient to handle eight horses strung out four and four, or 12 horses strung out four, four and four, than to handle them abreast. Six and six is possible on some wide implements, but a more general practice is to string them out a little further and in ranks of not more than four abreast.

Overleaf

70 Harvesting in Wasco County, on the far west coast of Oregon. The dim outline of distant hills may just be seen; and the slopes tackled demanded a large number of horses. In the biggest and best teams, thirty-two mules were used. The driver has lines only for the leaders, and he keeps a box of stones handy for encouraging any laggards. The horses are hitched to each other by a system of 'tying in' and 'bucking back'

71 How the corn lands of
North America were won.
Huge acreages and few men
called for big teams, and
Shire stallions were imported
in large numbers to add
weight to the offspring of
available mares

The true line of draught on a plough is the point at which the plough will
operate with least exertion to the team. Side draught is caused by the
tendency of the plough to twist sideways, which is due to hitching away from
the true line of draught. If the plough is twisting, the furrow wheels are set at
angles to hold the plough straight. This causes increased friction, which
increases draught. Side draught is also caused if any horse exerts a pull in a
direction other than that in which its body moves.

At several stations tests have been made using dynamometers, which can
accurately measure the number of pounds' pull required to move a plough
under any circumstances. Tests with integrating dynamometers behind
each line of horses have shown that the amount of draught exerted by each
pair is exactly the same whether they are the lead, the swing (second) or the
wheel pair.

Farmers disapproving of the tandem hitch claim that they cannot work as
close to the hedge, as more turning space is needed. The horses trample the
ground more in turning, and power is lost through being further from the
implement. The first and second objections can be overcome by round-and-
round working. The third does not apply to ploughs, though it does apply to
stone-boats or logs with friction along the length of the base.

The enormous pressure exerted by a large team of good Shires makes it
imperative that chains are strong. An eight-horse team walking at three
miles an hour could exert a strain of 12,000 pounds, or from five to six tons.

When big teams of three ranks or more are used, the minimum field size is
reckoned to be 40 acres. A great many arable fields in Britain have been
enlarged to at least that since 1945. The big team takes a little longer to turn
at the corners, but because of the large implements used, turns are only half
as frequent as with smaller teams and narrower implements.

To those of us whose introduction to horses was via the entirely practical
waggoners and foremen of our home villages, the amount of science applied
to horse teams comes as a constant surprise. After Brunel, American colleges
early this century did valuable research which was applied by the down-to-
earth teamsters who drove the big teams.

In 1917 Wayne Dinsmore journeyed across America from New England to the West. He found that the New Englanders ploughed only an acre a day, because they used small horses of 900 to 1,000 pounds, or a little over half the weight of a good Shire. In Pennsylvania a three-horse hitch turned over two to two-and-a-half acres a day, but in Oregon and Washington nine to ten acres a day was average. Three-furrow ploughs hauled by teams of eight to ten in tandem were the reason.

Wayne Dinsmore prevailed upon Dr E.A. White, of the University of Illinois, to use the dynamometer on which he had been working for three years to carry out tests of draught. It was found that the ordinary four-abreast hitch was inefficient, as it was impossible to eliminate side draught unless part of the team walked on the ploughed ground, which of course was impractical. The side draught was from 15 to 35 per cent, and occurred even with three abreast. In a 'strung-out' team it was eliminated, and the ploughs did better work.

With a big team in tandem, the line of draught tended to rise. The pull was at too high a point on the collars of the first three horses, causing them discomfort and lowering efficiency. By means of weighting, the line of draught was lowered to its correct place, and the horses quietened down and returned fresh at night. As Wayne Dinsmore said to an engineers' gathering in 1920:

This is the first step in increasing the efficiency of horse labour. The second is to increase the efficiency of the horses. As soon as you give us research showing how much less efficient the little horses are than the 1,700- and 1,800-pound horses, you will see the most rapid improvement in horse-breeding.

This was the purpose of all those Shire stallions that crossed the Atlantic – to add weight to the scrub teams that of necessity made up the numbers. And what numbers they were. In 1890 there were 18 million horses on American farms. In 1920 there were 26 million, and still more than ten million in 1947.

Reginald L. Ottley described one of the greatest of the 'big teams' in *The*

72 An example of the mixed sorts available to pull this early corn drill in North America

Listener, June 1960. He had been travelling across inland Australia on a big bay riding horse, to escape from an area flooded by six weeks of constant rain.

As he reached the point where the bridge should have been, he found a table-top waggon and 14 tons of wool, bogged down. It was in the charge of 'Yacka', an experienced bushman. Its own 18 horses and 18 from another waggon in the convoy of four had failed to move it. So the teams from all the waggons, 76 horses in all, were being yoked to it; and being yoked more than belly deep in swirling, muddy flood waters.

'Yacka' arranged them the way he wanted: a pair of his own, then several pairs of the other teamsters' horses. Placing them in that manner, he had horses that knew his voice all along the great team. Waggon teams are driven by voice, not with reins.

The horses became restless. They wanted to swing their rumps to the rain. We had to squeeze in between them to get to their heads. Some lashed out, others bumped us with their ribs. No team horse is ever fully broken; he is only taught to lead, and have a collar, blinkers and chains slipped on him. For the rest, he is left pretty much to himself – never has his feet picked up, or anything like that. Shoes are an unknown quantity.

Eventually the huge team was lined up, and the leaders yoked. 'Yacka's' leaders were a gelding named Toby and a mare, Bonny. Both were massive, in a raw-boned way. 'Yacka' told them to ease up, and in so doing stretched out the team until, inch by inch, every horse was standing straight, settled into his collar.

Then 'Yacka's' voice boomed again. 'Toby! Bonny! Wedge up there. Wedge up there, or I'll dust your hides.' Slowly; so slowly you could see him twitch with the strain, Toby heaved in his collar. Bonny did the same. Behind them, one after the other, the rest of the team dipped their heads. Hoof by sucking hoof, they strained forward.

The waggon began to roll, surging through the flood, with a crest on its prow. 'Yacka' kept the team going.

His voice urged them; coaxed them; swore at them. But you could feel his love for the horses, straining under his urging. Then, suddenly, the waggon rolled freely. It had reached hard ground, and its weight was nothing for the great team. Pounding through the water, they almost bolted. But 'Yacka's' great voice held them, eased them down slowly. Prick-eared under the calling, Toby and Bonny eased their pulling. The team behind them slackened off, too, without tangling their chains.

Such stories are a tribute to the great lead horses, of Shires and other breeds, that first cultivated the New World. They have no memorials. Yet without their understanding and intelligent reactions, the massed power behind them would have been useless. I hope some fellow writer in those wide countries can set down their feats, before they are lost and buried by the hundred-horse power, soul-less tractor.

13 Owning a Shire

Buying

When buying a Shire for the first time, a great many factors require consideration. The needs of the owner-groom are very different from those of the company establishing a stable under the care of an experienced horseman. Breeding brings in yet another dimension.

The dearest class of animal is the filly foal. The cheapest is the colt foal of only moderate quality. Where funds are limited, there is a temptation to buy the latter, and hope that it will grow out well.

The snag with this aspiration is that the cost of the foal is only the start of

73 A Shire foal finds the world a pleasant place. (*Audrey Hart*)

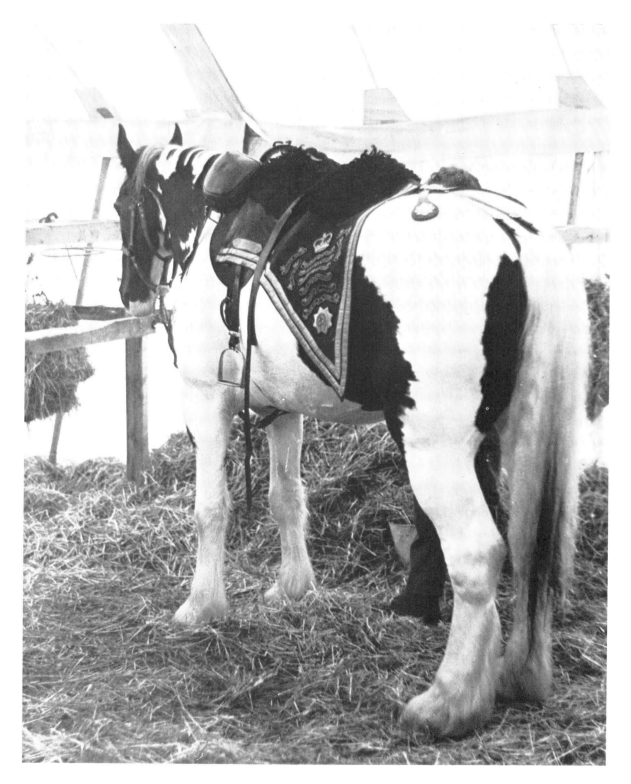

the expenses. With any class of stock, a good one costs no more in feed than a poor one, and to rear a foal through its first and second winter demands concentrate or cereal feeding. In the foreseeable future, concentrates will not be cheap.

A colt is often a low price because he is not a popular colour. The adage that 'No good horse was ever a bad colour' does not withstand modern showfield opinion. If the foal has a splatch of white where he shouldn't, that white area will grow as the foal grows.

There is the temptation to think that a foal with a lot of white or roan will make a drum horse. He might. But even if he is suitable, a regiment requires only one, not three or four. So the market is limited. Temperament is vital, and many potential drum horses fail the very exacting temperament tests.

British Army horse authorities invariably have their wits about them, and know where the best coloured horses are to be found. They usually have their eyes on suitable candidates long before they are needed, so the dream of buying a 'mis-marked' Shire and ending up with a four-figure drum horse is unrealistic.

Such a horse, properly broken and nicely mannered, would probably find a home in a single turnout. Prices paid tend to be little above killing price, however, and £700 or £800 is not much recompense for two or three years' keep even if the foal cost £200 or even less.

The brewers remain the best customers for geldings. They need quality; large, well-made horses of suitable action, and sound colour to match their existing teams are pre-requisites. To attain these aims involves purchasing a colt in which others have seen potential. The initial cost is greater, and the

Left

74 This attractive piebald drum horse makes one regret the passing of that colour from the Shire registry

75 The 'unicorn' is a difficult hitch to drive. The leader is out on his own, with no pal to keep him company, and he is at some distance from the coachman. Ind Coope feel fortunate to have found a quite exceptional leader in Regent (left foreground.) (*Audrey Hart*)

76 Thwaites' Shires are Major and Royal, the groomsmen Eric Longson and David Clarkson, and the occasion the Witton Park Parade, Blackburn, Lancashire. The managing director of Thwaites Brewery, Blackburn, is David Kay, Hon. Treasurer of the Shire Horse Society and a staunch advocate of the draught horse for city work. (*Thwaites, Blackburn*)

77 Shire breeder Arthur Lewis of Tamworth-in-Arden, Warwickshire, handling a part-bred two-year-old. Her dam was by the Shire stallion Ladbrook What's Wanted out of a seven-eighths hunter mare, and her sire was a strong-boned Thoroughbred. She is the class of horse that always commands a premium, whether as heavyweight hunter, eventer or police horse

colt must be well fed throughout his young life if he is to realize that potential.

Animals that work well together do command a premium, more so with the growing interest in ploughing matches. Here again, horsemen like to have something that not only *is* good, but *looks* good. To purchase an apparently cheap colt foal is to risk the heartbreak of rearing it expensively, getting to know it, and then seeing it go to the meat trade.

A better buy is a two-year-old. At this age potential is more certainly assessed, and the two very expensive first winters are passed.

Sound legs and sound feet are essentials. Hoof colour does not matter, though blue hoofs are associated with hardness, and shelly or splitting hoofs should be avoided. Length between toe and heel is needed, and the heels must not be flat, or frog trouble may ensue. On older horses a cannon bone measurement of nine to ten inches is expected. A broad knee, a straight foreleg and a sloping shoulder are required. Don't forget that a solid collar bed is required in a draught horse, whose forelegs should be set well underneath the shoulders.

A tail set well up the back gives a smart appearance to any horse. Too much dip in the back is a weakness, as are 'sickle hocks' that have undue curve. Girth is vital. The Shire must be deep through its chest; this depth is one of the first things to catch the judge's eye as the horses first enter the ring, and if it is absent the judge may not look that way again. The Shire mare has a longer rib cage and a more slender neck than the stallion. But she must still look like a cart horse and not like one of the 'kipper-ribbed' varieties!

A pointed ear makes a horse look alert, and often denotes intelligence.

Though these neat ears are a bonus, the Shire's head must never look 'pony-fied'.

Action is most important. At the walk and the trot the legs must move in a straight line, neither swinging in nor dishing out, and this applies whether the horse is seen from in front or behind.

Above all, when buying a Shire, take with you someone you can trust who knows the Shire world and its inhabitants, both equine and human, thoroughly. A buyer who relies solely on knowledge gleaned from a book is foolish, and sooner rather than later he will be 'stuck', and find the process very expensive.

78 English summer. A local show at Gorefield, Cambridgeshire, with Shire classes that would grace a county event

The Show Animal

Today's Shire is the show animal *par excellence*. It has a wide range of colours that transforms the show ring into a major spectacle. The feather on its free-flowing legs gives a flashy appearance, and the extra height of the 'big 'uns' commands awe and respect from people more familiar with pony sizes.

Although Shire exhibitors make less of a cult of feather than do the Clydesdale men, the fine and usually contrasting white feather of the modern Shire certainly sets off the animal. In the show ring, discussions about the link between bone and feather have little meaning. Appearances count, and that flow of feather from an eight-up team like that of Young's or Samuel Smith's Brewery cannot be surpassed as a spectacle.

Suffolk and Percheron have as much action as the Shire – their exhibitors would claim more! – but their clean legs do not mark them out so clearly and

quickly to the uninitiated. Suffolks are limited to chesnut, though in several shades, while Percherons are either grey or black, again with several shades of the former. The Shire may be grey, brown, bay or black, with widely variable amounts of white on the blaze, and the range of white legs from none to four. So there is immediately more to see for the general, fee-paying public.

However, the public do not like the shaven tail, and the sooner the Shire world rids itself of that abhorrence the better. Tails may still be plaited in a variety of ways, with the 'jug handle' a breed feature.

Starting from either side of the top of the tail, a piece the thickness of a finger is plaited, bringing in raffia. Two rather thinner plaits are made down either side of and above the first, using plenty of raffia so that they stand as upright pencils.

The 'jug handle' is then affixed to the first plait, and tied round with raffia. Coloured ribbons are tied in, dangling down about eight inches, and finishing as a fishtail. The rest of the hair is then combed down.

A Shire mane is carefully combed to one side of the neck. The bass or raffia is laid on the neck from a point just behind the ears, and secured with a few hairs. Plaiting proceeds by taking in only a proportion of the mane, the rest of the hair being combed down the side. This is unlike the Suffolk style, which incorporates the whole of the mane into the plait.

Legs are washed with white soap in hot water, or with some 'secret' concoction of the exhibitor's own devising. A recent Shire Horse Society ruling bars the use of any additives to 'set' the hair above the hoofs.

Care and Kindness

Shires may live for 20 or 30 years or even more. There comes a time when even the best horse's day is done, and what then? This is a question that every budding Shire owner must be prepared to face, and the same applies to every other class of stock.

It may be argued that when a horse comes to the end of its useful life, either as breeder or worker, then it is entitled to spend its remaining years in familiar surroundings among people – and horses – that it knows and trusts.

This is not practical where a large number of horses is kept. An establishment with six or eight brood mares and geldings probably has two or three up-and-coming youngsters as well, and if all its horses were pensioned off when they had ceased to breed or work, that could add another three or four to the total.

The plain fact is that few owners can afford to do this. For the majority, it would entail keeping fewer younger horses. Most genuine stockmen decide to have the horse put down when the time comes.

The responsibility does not end with that decision. The horse should be taken to a licensed slaughterer after proper arrangements have been made, and the owner must accompany his old favourite. He must not leave the horse to others who may have become callous through the constant pressure of work. He must see the job through. To dodge it because he was fond of the old animal is the cruellest of partings.

There are 'rest homes' for old horses, but whether they are of benefit to

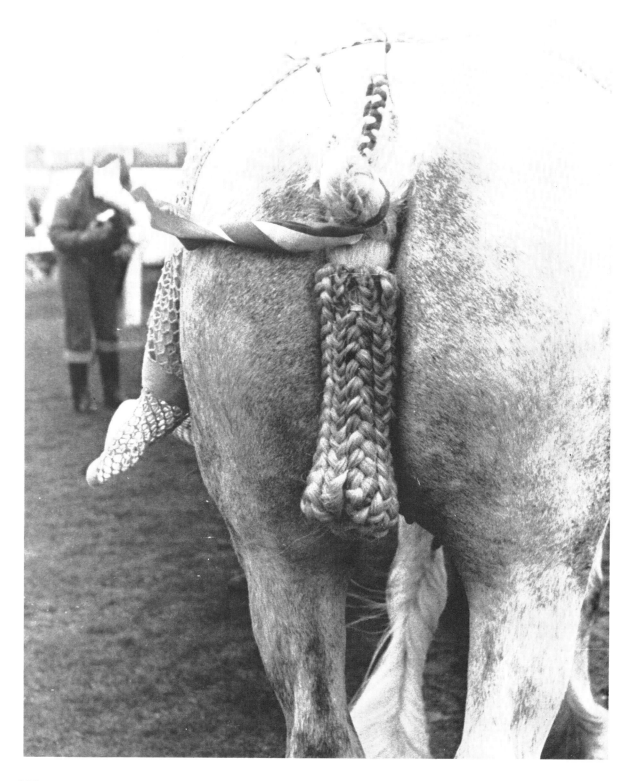

the horses is debatable. The horse is taken to a strange place, among strange people and strange neighbours, to do nothing. Its previous owner has lost control of it. Attendants may change, not always for the better.

The Royal Society for the Prevention of Cruelty to Animals

In the days of the great slaughter of farm horses during the 1940s and '50s, there was a strong case for rescuing strong young Shires from the slaughterer, and keeping them in the hope that times would improve.

The R.S.P.C.A. did a good job here. It has maintained a Home of Rest for Horses for over half a century, first on the Isle of Wight and then at Milton Keynes, in association with the Wyndham Cottle bequest. Heavy-horse pensioners are sometimes found there, and the Bristol coach horse Theo is a resident. Another long-established home is also based in Buckinghamshire, at Speen, Aylesbury.

Left
81 One of several ways of dressing a full length Shire tail. (*Audrey Hart*)

82 Two young Shires with nicely plaited tails. The neck ribbon enhances the female's long, graceful neck

R.S.P.C.A. involvement with the heavy horse goes back a long way. In 1898 it persuaded the Board of Agriculture (forerunner of the present Ministry) to intervene in the export trade. The Society claims that if its recommendations had been fully implemented at the time, much unnecessary suffering over the next half century could have been avoided.

The first R.S.P.C.A. horse brasses were awarded in 1895, according to the late Arthur Moss, who chronicled the Society's activities. The R.S.P.C.A. was associated with the London Cart Horse Parade since its inception, and also applied for a site in Battersea Park to hold the second show in 1896.

For the first ten years diplomas were awarded, and the practice of providing brasses went on until 1972.

A special revival of the custom took place in Jubilee Year, 1977, through the enthusiastic efforts of an R.S.P.C.A. staff member. The very rare merit brasses were issued in 1907.

R.S.P.C.A. brasses are especially treasured by the heavy-horse fraternity. They cannot be bought from the R.S.P.C.A. They are awarded only for a particular achievement. Another special award commemorated the first televising of the London Cart-Horse Parade, which incidentally included

Left
83 Showing teaches a young foal a great deal, not least how to enter a trailer alongside its mother without fear. (*Audrey Hart*)

84 There may be better ways of spending a summer afternoon than among the Shires, but scenes like these make them difficult to imagine. (*Audrey Hart*)

van horses from 1890 to 1903, after which they held their own very
admirable event.

During World War Two, merit badges were manufactured of white metal
or even plastic, because of the shortage of suitable alternatives. Now that the
Shire horse is re-emerging as a much sought-after animal for work and
pleasure, we may be sure that the R.S.P.C.A. will play its full part in
encouraging correct, kind management.

The post-World War Two decline in the use of horses for draught

purposes led to marked problems with surplus animals.

The continuing export of old and worn-out horses, mainly to Continental markets, was no credit to the country. R.S.P.C.A. protests about the practice were at a peak when World War One ended. With Miss Cole, an individual member, the campaign continued through the inter-war period.

The R.S.P.C.A. was instrumental in securing the first 'minimum values' Order in 1937, which helped restrict exports to animals sold for work, sport or breeding, and therefore likely to be properly cared for.

86 Harness details on Courage Shires. The horse on the right has his rein buckled to his Liverpool bit ring, indicating that he is easily driven. His partner requires rather more leverage on the bit. These are the type of Shires that attracted 900,000 visitors to the Centre

By 1945 the minimum price levels had become unrealistic and ineffective. Not until 1950 was a new Order drafted to meet the new conditions, in which the minimum value of heavy horses for export was set at £80. This followed the Rosebery Committee of Inquiry, prompted by R.S.P.C.A. sponsorship of a Commons measure to improve the situation. In 1979 the figure rose to £715, the value suggested by the R.S.P.C.A. to the Ministry of Agriculture to correspond with the change in money values.

In 1960, disclosure of continuing exports of live horses from Ireland led to the petitioning of the Irish government by one-and-a-quarter million people, led by the R.S.P.C.A. and a popular newspaper.

14 The Future

The Shire's long and dignified history appeared to be coming to an end in the late 1950s. Thanks to the imaginative and strenuous efforts of enthusiasts, its future has now been secured for many years. But what shape will that future take?

The great horses are now kept primarily for pleasure as well as for profit. Sometimes there is only a thin line of distinction between the two, but the Shire is one of the few farm stock to retain the place that all animals once had for past generations of farmers. Farming to them was a complete life, and they needed no interests beyond their cattle, sheep and pigs, their crops, and the horses that cultivated those crops.

87 A Devon Shire Horse Farm Centre gelding, Roy, attracts all eyes (*Western Morning News Co. Ltd*

Today, farming with its sophisticated equipment, small or non-existent paid labour force, and cash flow problems, is much like any other industry. Its participants will feel more and more the need for an absorbing yet relaxing hobby away from their daily routine, and the Shire fulfils this need admirably.

Though the farmer is best placed to keep heavy horses for obvious reasons – corn, hay, grazing and stabling all to hand – people from many other walks of life contrive means of keeping a Shire, even if on another's land. Hoteliers, garage owners, veterinary surgeons and transport managers are amongst Shire owners.

For the show ring, in either the in-hand or turnout classes, size is likely to count. In America a team of matched Belgians stretching to 19 hands is worth a great deal of money. In the horse's hey-day as a carriage animal, the Yorkshire Coach Horse was developed from the Cleveland Bay by infusions of large-type Thoroughbred blood. When a really good Yorkshire Coach Horse was produced, it was the flashiest, most striking example of equine beauty on the London streets.

88 Green trees, Shire mares and foals under an August sun make a timeless scene. (*Audrey Hart*)

W. Scarth Dixon wrote before World War One:

The 'Beaux of the Regency' took it into their heads that it was the 'correct thing' to drive a cabriolet on high wheels, drawn by a tall blood-like horse and with a diminutive and impudent 'tiger' hanging on the straps behind. The taller the horse and the more diminutive and impudent the 'tiger' the happier the voluminous neck-clothed beau who held the ribbons. Of course Fashion's whims must be gratified, and the want being proclaimed, dealers set their wits to work to find the horses and breeders to breed them. The tallest Cleveland Bay mares were selected and mated to the tallest Thoroughbred stallions, and tall, narrow, split-up horses were soon bred.

He goes on to say that this absurd craze inflicted a severe blow on the Cleveland Bay breed, and one from which it has never fully recovered. Shire breeders should take warning from history, and not go for height and forget all else.

All horsemen know that the outsize animal is the more liable to strains and disorders, especially of the legs and feet. Indeed, W. Scarth Dixon expounds on this very point: 'One drawback to the tall horses with long arched neck was that so many of them developed roaring and kindred diseases. When they brought high prices the risk might be run, and indeed was run, but it is useless running risks for an exploded fashion.'

89 From horses to tractors and back again. This trailer is adapted for horses through the Pinney hitch cart, being converted to a four-wheel rulley. The horse is an Ardennes, the Shire's latest rival from across the Channel

It is most gratifying to see increased entries in turnout classes, partly as a result of financial inducements from the show societies. This extra competitiveness will make the production of a winning team even harder, with more and more incentives to go for the big horses. If other points are kept in proportion, this may work, but going for height alone cannot benefit the Shire breed in the long run.

The taller the horse, the higher the point of draught. Thus the compact Suffolk or Ardennes has an advantage over the tall Shire when pulling. This is more important where an implement going in or over the ground is concerned, for very tall horses tend to raise the point of the plough through the angle of their trace chains.

The dray with its large wheels and raised pulling points is better suited to the big animal. But he will be more expensive to keep, and will need special harness which is already a costly item.

Such strictures from a commentator on the heavy-horse scene will be little heeded when matings are planned and effected. The value of the resulting foal is the crux, and if a market develops for really tall Shires, it will be met.

This size in the Shire was one reason for importing Ardennes horses from across the Channel. They are low-slung, and thrive on coarser rations. The cost of corn is high, and indeed its use at all in animal rations is being questioned at a time when so many humans are starving through want of it.

90 A heavier part-bred, probably half Shire, at the annual Midlands Foal Sale, Bingley Hall, Stafford. For small holder's or light carting work, this type is unbeatable

The Ardennes is reputed to live on grass or hay, and to do well on more exposed ground.

The initiative of Charles Pinney and others in importing horse-drawn farm machinery from Poland, and manufacturing their own, is resolving the chicken-and-egg situation under which farmers could not use their horses on the land because they had no implements, and manufacturers would make none because of the unknown demand.

It is claimed that horses will return first to the poorer marginal areas. This I doubt. The hill and upland farmers were and are knowledgable cattle and sheep breeders, and I would turn to them unfailingly for information on those classes of stock. For heavy-horse lore I would travel the lowland, arable districts.

The tractor's function on upland farms is often transporting feed and fencing materials from one point to another, which may be some miles away. Here the tractor's extra speed has the edge.

The Shire team has a distinct advantage in one respect. Many accidents have occurred through tractors running away and overturning on steep slopes; horses are positively safer. They can be yoked into big teams to pull most implements, and regain their energy on easier going after a long, uphill haul.

One thing is certain: where Shires are returning as work animals, it is because their owners *like* them. I know of no case of a person with an in-built dislike of horses returning to literal horse power on purely economic grounds.

91 A Shire does a useful job delivering milk in a Northamptonshire village

Appendices

1 City Haulage in the 1980s

In October 1981, the Shire Horse Society published a report on Heavy Horse Haulage in the 1980s. Its investigation was carried out by Ian C. Webster B.A. (Econ.), under the direction of a Committee of the Society, Messrs. D.J. Simonds, J.D. Kay, W.A. Gilbey and R.E.S. Davey.

The report compares heavy horse haulage costs with those of motor transport, over short distances. The term 'heavy horses' is intended to refer to good working specimens of the Shire, Suffolk, Clydesdale or British Percheron breeds.

Some interesting basic principles were laid down concerning the physical capacity of heavy horses.

1 Payload It is generally accepted that a reasonable load for a heavy horse is twice its own weight. Thus the payload for a pair of horses working abreast is four tons. This unit is the basis of the investigation. A single horse needs the services of one driver for only two tons, and is therefore less economic.

2 Distance A horse can travel ten to twelve miles a day without hardship.

3 Hours of work Eight hours a day is the maximum where heavy loads are concerned. Companies co-operating with the investigation work horses for only six hours daily, on a five-day week. This amounts to 240 days a year, but horses can easily work a six-day week if necessary.

4 Speed The heavy horse is unsuitable where speed is important (e.g. emergency services, public transport). Nor is it suited to a small payload and infrequent stops.

5 Terrain Though horses are not suited to steep hills, those found in the average town do not present problems. Vaux Brewery horses operate on some fairly steep inclines in Sunderland.

6 Weather very rarely affects the work of horses in towns. If properly shod with 'frost nails' to give extra grip, they have in fact advantages over motors in very cold conditions where windscreens freeze and batteries fail to function.

7 Summary Businesses that could use horses are those where the payload does not exceed four tons, where deliveries are within a five-mile radius and where speed is secondary or is limited by the environment. In such short-haul transport, the ratio of standing time to running time is high.

2 Standard of Points for Shires

A scale of points for the breed has been carefully drawn up and this has been amended when necessary, to meet the modern requirements. For instance, years ago, a great characteristic of the Shire was the wealth of hair, or feather, on the legs. Today the demand is for a cleaner-legged horse, with straight, fine, silky hair.

The standard of points laid down by the Council is as follows:

Stallions

Colour Black, brown, bay or grey. No good stallion should be splashed with large white patches over the body. He should not be roan or chestnut.

Height Minimum 16.2 hands and upwards. Average about 17.2 hands.

Head Long and lean, neither too large nor too small, with long neck in proportion to the body. Large jaw bone should be avoided.

Eyes Large, well set and docile expression. Wall eye to be avoided if possible.

Nose Nostrils thin and wide; lips together and slightly Roman.

Ears Long, lean, sharp and sensitive.

Throat Clean cut and lean.

Shoulder Deep and oblique, wide enough to support the collar.

Neck Long, slightly arched, well set on to give the horse a commanding appearance.

Girth The girth varies from 6 feet to 8 feet in stallions of from 16.2 to 18 hands.

Back Short, strong and muscular. Should not be dipped or roached.

Loins Standing well up, denoting good constitution (must not be flat).

Fore-end Wide across the chest, with legs well under the body and well enveloped in muscle, or action is impeded.

Hind-quarters Long and sweeping, wide and full of muscle, well let down towards the thighs.

Ribs Round, deep and well sprung, not flat.

Forelegs Should be as straight as possible down to pastern.

Hindlegs Hocks should not be too far back and in line with the hindquarters with ample width broadside and narrow in front. 'Puffy' and 'sickle' hocks should be avoided. The leg sinews should be clean cut and hard like fine cords to touch, and clear of short cannon bone.

Bone measurement Of flat bone 11 inches is ample, although occasionally 12½ inches is recorded – flat bone is heavier and stronger than spongey bone. Hocks must be broad, deep and flat, and set at the correct angle for leverage.

Feet Deep, solid and wide, with thick open walls. Coronets should be hard and sinewy with substance.

Hair Not too much, fine, straight and silky.

A good Shire stallion should stand from 16.2 hands upwards, and weigh from 18 to 22 hundredweight when matured, without being overdone in condition. He should possess a masculine head, and a good crest with sloping, not upright, shoulders running well into the back, which should be short and well coupled with the loins. The tail should be well set up, and not what is known as 'goose-rumped'. Both head and tail should be carried erect. The ribs should be well sprung, not flat sided, with good middle, which generally denotes good constitution. A stallion should have good feet and joints; the feet should be wide and big around the top of the coronets with sufficient length in the pasterns. When in motion, he should move with force using both knees and hocks, and the latter should be kept close together; he should be straight and true before and behind.

Modification or Variation of Stallion Standard of Points for Mares

Colour Black, brown, bay, grey, roan and chestnut.

Height 16 hands upwards.

Head Long and lean, neither too large nor too small, long neck in proportion to the body, but of feminine appearance.

Neck Long and slightly arched, and not of masculine appearance.

Girth 5 feet to 7 feet (matured) according to size and age of animal.

Back legs Strong and in some instances longer than a male. Short, with short cannons.

Bone measurement 9 to 11 inches of flat bone, with clean cut sinews.

A mare should be of high quality, long and deep with free action, of a feminine and matronly appearance, standing from 16 hands and upwards on short legs; she should have plenty of room to carry her foal.

Modification or Variation of Stallion Standard of Points for Geldings

Colour As for mares.

Height 16.2 hands and upwards.

Girth From 6 feet to 7 feet 6 inches.

Bone measurement 10 to 11 inches under knee, slightly more under hock and broadside on, of flat hard quality.

A gelding should be upstanding, thick, well-balanced, very active and a lively mover; he should be full of courage, and should look and be capable of doing a full day's work. Geldings weigh from 17 to 22 hundredweight.

Guidelines

These notes have in no way been prepared to reflect the way in which judges behave or carry out their work, but merely as guidelines, particularly for younger judges in answer to questions raised with the Society.

(a) Horses with unclipped tails should not be penalized.

(b) Bevil shoes. Horse shown without bevil shoes should not be penalized.

3 Local Societies

ABERGELE & DISTRICT SHIRE HORSE SOCIETY (Secretary H. Thomas Esq., J.P.) Garnedd, Llanfairfechan, Gwynedd.

DERBYSHIRE AGRICULTURAL & HORTICULTURAL SOCIETY (Secretary B.G. Daykin Esq.) 17 Chestnut Avenue, Mickleover, Derby.

GREAT ECCLESTON SHIRE HORSE SOCIETY (Secretary T. Kay Esq.) 2 Park Lane, Wesham, Nr. Kirkham, Preston, Lancashire.

LICHFIELD SHIRE HORSE SOCIETY (Secretary R.F. Schoffham Esq.) St. Mary's Chambers, Lichfield, Staffordshire.

LINCOLNSHIRE SHIRE HORSE ASSOCIATION (Secretary B.A. Neave Esq.) School Lane, Grayingham, Lincolnshire.

MOBBERLY & DISTRICT SHIRE HORSE SOCIETY (Secretary F.R. Marshall Esq.) 36 Hawthorn Avenue, Wilmslow, Cheshire.

MONTGOMERYSHIRE ENTIRE HORSE SOCIETY (Secretaries Messrs. Morris, Marshall & Poole) Coach Chambers, Welshpool, Powys.

NORTH YORKSHIRE HEAVY HORSE SOCIETY (Secretary A. Jenkins Esq.) East Side Farm, Staintondale, Scarborough, North Yorkshire.

SOUTH WEST YORKSHIRE SHIRE HORSE HIRING SOCIETY
(Secretary H. Lewis Esq.) Goodyfield Farm, Tofts
Lane, Rivelin, Sheffield, South Yorkshire.
WESSEX SHIRE HORSE HIRING SOCIETY (Secretary F.W.
Cooper Esq.) Skinners Farm, Woolland, Blandford,
Dorset.
WISBECH SHIRE HORSE SOCIETY (Secretary R.K. Reeve
Esq.) Agriculture House, 33a Alexandra Road,
Wisbech, Cambridgeshire, PE13 1HS.
YORKSHIRE SHIRE HORSE SOCIETY (Secretary W.H.
Chambers Esq.) Trinity House Farm, Swanland
Dale, North Ferriby, East Yorkshire.

American Addresses
CALIFORNIA DRAFT HORSE ASSOCIATION (Secretary
Barbara Patison) PO Box 157, Penryn, California
95663.
DRAFT HORSE & MULE ASSOCIATION OF AMERICA
(Executive Secretary Miles McCarry) 521 Elden
Drive, Cary, Illinois 60013.
KANSAS DRAFT HORSE & MULE ASSOCIATION (President
Harold Tonn) Valley View Ranch, Haven, Kansas
67543.
NEW YORK STATE DRAFT HORSE CLUB (Lee Waite) RD
1, Box 122, Edmeston, New York 13335.
NORTH CAROLINA DRAFT HORSE & MULE ASSOCIATION
(Dr E.D. Richards) Box 386, Salisbury, North
Carolina 28144.
SOUTH DAKOTA DRAFT HORSE & MULE BREEDERS
ASSOCIATION (Vice President Jerry Adrian) Colonial
Acres, Rt 3, Sioux Falls, South Dakota.
WASHINGTON DRAFT HORSE & MULE ASSOCIATION
(Secretary Cheryl Wilder) 7931 Valley View Road,
Custer, Washington 9824C.

4 List of Shows with Shire Classes
The shows are listed in the order in which they take
place – actual dates vary from year to year.

March
NATIONAL SHIRE HORSE SHOW, Peterborough,
Cambridgeshire

April
LLEYN & DISTRICT AGRICULTURAL SHOW, Gwynedd
LONDON HARNESS HORSE PARADE
THE PAGEANT OF THE HORSE (Doncaster Racecourse)

May
NEWARK & NOTTINGHAMSHIRE COUNTY SHOW
ROYAL WINDSOR HORSE SHOW
BATLEY HORSE SHOW, West Yorkshire
SHROPSHIRE & WEST MIDLANDS SHOW
DEVON COUNTY SHOW
HEATHFIELD AGRICULTURAL SHOW, Sussex
OTLEY SHOW, West Yorkshire
TERRINGTON ST CLEMENT HEAVY HORSE SHOW, Norfolk

HERTFORDSHIRE SHOW
MONTGOMERYSHIRE COUNTY SHOW
CHARLTON PARK SHOW, Wiltshire
DERBYSHIRE COUNTY SHOW
MALLING HORSE SHOW, Kent
WOODHALL SPA & DISTRICT AGRICULTURAL SHOW,
Lincolnshire
WARRINGTON HORSE SOCIETY, Lancashire
STAFFORDSHIRE COUNTY SHOW
SUFFOLK SHOW
ALL ENGLAND JUMPING COURSE, Sussex

June
MESSINGHAM SHOW
ROYAL BATH & WEST, Shepton Mallet, Somerset
LEYLAND SHIRE HORSE SHOW, Lancashire
DEEPING SHOW, Peterborough, Cambridgeshire
ROYAL CORNWALL
SOUTH OF ENGLAND SHOW, Ardingly, Sussex
ESSEX COUNTY SHOW, Chelmsford
GOREFIELD SHOW, Wisbech, Cambridgeshire
ABERYSTWYTH AGRICULTURAL SHOW
THREE COUNTIES SHOW, Malvern, Worcestershire
LONDON BOROUGH OF WANDSWORTH
CHESHIRE COUNTY AGRICULTURAL SHOW
LINCOLNSHIRE SHOW
HILLINGDON SHOW SOCIETY, Buckinghamshire
LETCHWORTH, BALDOCK & DISTRICT RIDING CLUB,
Hertfordshire

July
ROYAL NORFOLK SHOW
WINTERTON AGRICULTURAL SHOW, Scunthorpe, South
Humberside
SEATON ROSS SHOW, York
THE ROYAL SHOW, National Agricultural Centre,
Stoneleigh, Kenilworth, Warwickshire
SOUTHAMPTON SHOW
CITY OF HEREFORD SHOW
PUDSEY BOROUGH SHOW, West Yorkshire
MARKET BOSWORTH ANNUAL HORSE SHOW, Staffordshire
SOUTH HUMBERSIDE COUNTY SHOW
GREAT YORKSHIRE SHOW, Harrogate, North Yorkshire
KENT COUNTY SHOW, Maidstone
MANCHESTER SHOW
SWANSEA VALLEY SHOW SOCIETY
SNAITH SHOW, Goole, Yorkshire
ALREWAS & DISTRICT AGRICULTURAL SOCIETY,
Burton-on-Trent, Staffordshire
NEWPORT SHOW, Shropshire
GREAT ECCLESTON & DISTRICT AGRICULTURAL SHOW, St
Michaels-on-Wyre, Preston, Lancashire
SPILSBY & DISTRICT SHOW, Boston, Lincolnshire
TATTON WEEK-END EVENT, Knutsford, Cheshire
ASHBY DE LA ZOUCH & DISTRICT AGRICULTURAL SHOW,
Leicestershire
THE ROYAL INTERNATIONAL HORSE SHOW
ROYAL WELSH, Builth Wells

EAST OF ENGLAND SHOW, Peterborough, Cambridgeshire
ABERGAVENNY & BORDER COUNTIES, Gwent
HECKINGTON SHOW, Sleaford, Lincolnshire
PONSANOOTH HEAVY HORSE SHOW, Truro, Cornwall
WOOLLEY HORSE SHOW, Wakefield, Yorkshire
PWLLHELI AGRICULTURAL SHOW, Gwynedd
RYEDALE SHOW, North Yorkshire
ROYAL LANCASHIRE AGRICULTURAL SOCIETY
NANTWICH & SOUTH CHESHIRE SHOW
NEW FOREST SHOW
OSWESTRY SHOW
FULMER IN-HAND SHOW, Buckinghamshire
ST HELENS SHOW, Merseyside
EMBASSY JULY INTERNATIONAL ALL ENGLAND JUMPING COURSE, Hickstead, Surrey
HULL SHOW

August

PENMORFA & DISTRICT SHOW, Gwynedd
DUDLEY TOWN ANNUAL SHOW, West Midlands
TALYGARN & PONTYCLUN HORSE SHOW, Mid Glamorgan
DODINGTON HEAVY HORSE SHOW, Avon
RUTLAND SHOW
SYKEHOUSE SHOW SOCIETY, Goole, Yorkshire
HAREWOOD SHOW, Yorkshire
NEVERN SHOW, Dyfed
BAKEWELL SHOW, Derbyshire
HALIFAX SHOW
CANWELL SHOW, West Midlands
GARSTANG SHOW, Lancashire
EGLYSBACH & DISTRICT AGRICULTURAL & HORTICULTURAL SHOW, North Wales
ANGLESEY COUNTY SHOW
ST MELLONS SHOW, Gwent
UNITED COUNTIES SHOW, Dyfed
ASHBOURNE SHOW, Derbyshire
BEDWELLTY AGRICULTURAL SHOW, Gwent
PEMBROKESHIRE AGRICULTURAL SHOW
DENBIGHSHIRE & FLINTSHIRE AGRICULTURAL SOCIETY SHOW
MOBBERLY SHIRE HORSE SOCIETY IN CONJUNCTION WITH POYNTON SHOW, Cheshire
MID SOUTHERN COUNTIES AGRICULTURAL SHOW
MERIONETH AGRICULTURAL SOCIETY
EGTON HORSE & AGRICULTURAL SOCIETY, Whitby, North Yorkshire
ABERGELE & DISTRICT SHIRE HORSE OPEN DAY, Gwynedd
GREATER LONDON HORSE SHOW
DEARNE SHOW, Rotherham, South Yorkshire
KENILWORTH SHOW, Warwickshire
WOOLTON SHOW, Liverpool
HOPE SHOW, Derbyshire
ALTON SHOW, Hampshire
MOORGREEN SHOW, Nottingham
'WHITE HORSE' HEAVY HORSE SHOW, Oxfordshire

September

WALSALL SHOW, West Midlands
SHEFFIELD SHOW
KEIGHLEY SHOW, West Yorkshire
ORSETT SHOW, Essex
YESTERDAY'S FARMING, Taunton, Somerset
KINGSTON SHOW, Herefordshire
HENLEY AGRICULTURAL SHOW, Berkshire
NEWBURY AGRICULTURAL SHOW, Berkshire

October

MIDLAND SHIRE FOAL SHOW AND SALE, Bingley Hall, Stafford
BRITISH ISLES HORSE & TRACTOR PLOUGHING CHAMPIONSHIP, various venues
HORSE OF THE YEAR SHOW, Wembley Arena, London
BRAILSFORD & DISTRICT PLOUGHING & HEDGE CUTTING SOCIETY ANNUAL MATCH, Derby
WISBECH SHIRE HORSE SOCIETY SHOW & SALE, Gorefield, Cambridgeshire
CHESHIRE HORSE SALES, Tarporley, Cheshire
GREAT ALL ENGLAND PLOUGHING MATCH
NORTHERN HEAVY HORSE SOCIETY SHOW, York

No date is notified for the following but all have Shire classes:

BARNBY DUN AGRICULTURAL SOCIETY
BINGLEY SHOW
BOURNEMOUTH & WEST HANTS. HORSE SOCIETY
BURNLEY AGRICULTURAL SHOW
CHEPSTOW SHOW
COTSWOLD HARNESS HORSE & PONY SHOW
CUCKMERE VALLEY HORSE SHOW
ENFIELD & DISTRICT HORSE SOCIETY
GOOSNARGH & LONGRIDGE AGRICULTURAL SOCIETY
GREAT NORTHERN SHOW
GWENT COUNTY SHOW
HANNINGFIELD SHOW
HONITON & DISTRICT AGRICULTURAL ASSOCIATION
HONLEY AGRICULTURAL SHOW
KIMBOLTON COUNTY FAYRE (TILBROOK)
LANCASHIRE INTERNATIONAL HORSE SHOW
LEEK & DISTRICT SHOW SOCIETY
LEICESTER ADVERTISER PLOUGHING MATCH
LITTLEPORT SHOW
LLANRWST SHOW
LLANTWIT FARDRE SHOW
LONG SUTTON HEAVY HORSE SHOW
MIDLAND COUNTIES HORSE SHOW
MIDSHIRES EQUESTRIAN PROMOTIONS
MIDSHIRES HORSE SHOW
NORTH WALES SHOW
OHIO CLYDESDALE & SHIRE ASSOCIATION
ROYSTON & DISTRICT RIDING CLUB SHOW
SOUTH WEST DRIVING & HEAVY HORSE SHOW
SPRING WORKING SHOW

SUTTON DISTRICT AGRICULTURAL SOCIETY
THORPE PARK SHOW
TOTTINGTON & DISTRICT HORSE SHOW
WESTERN COUNTIES HEAVY HORSE SHOW
WHITTLESEY SHOW
WOKINGHAM & DISTRICT AGRICULTURAL SHOW

5 Shire Horse Society Winners

Champion Stallion, Mare and Gelding National Spring Show 1971–1982

1971
Stallion – Royston Harold 45335 – C.C. Etches, Brookfield Farm, Mickleover, Derby.
Mare – Burford Lady in White 139854 – H. Sutton, Burford Lane Farm, Lymm, Cheshire.
Gelding – Heaton Majestic – J. & W. Whewell Ltd, New Bridge Chemical Works, Radcliffe, Manchester.

1972
Stallion – Layston Conjuror 45393 – J. Russell, Church Farm, Barnsley, Gloucestershire.
Mare – Sleightwood Miss Fashion 139514 – T. Yates, Hall Farm, Windley, Derby.
Gelding – Heaton Majestic – J. & W. Whewell Ltd.

1973
Stallion – Royston Harold 45335 – C.C. Etches.
Mare – Burford Lady in White 139854 – H. Sutton. Esq.
Gelding – Whitley Superman – Arthur Wright Farms Ltd, Village Farm. Daresbury, Nr. Warrington, Lancashire.

1974
Stallion – Woodhouse Footprint 45442 – L. Fountain, Woodhouse Farm, Marston Montgomery, Derbyshire.
Mare – Wheelton Rose 139920 – Ll. Joseph & Sons, Grove Farm, Pyle, Nr. Bridgend, Glamorgan.
Gelding – Cowerslane David – T. Yates.

1975
Stallion – Hillmoor Enterprise 45392 – T.E. Moss, Hillmoor Farm, Eaton, Congleton, Cheshire.
Mare – Grange Wood Selina 139950 – T.W. Critchlow, Manor House Farm, Cubley, Ashbourne, Derbyshire.
Gelding – St Vincent's King William – Messrs. E. Coward Ltd, Bluebell Farm, Thorney, Peterborough.

1976
Stallion – Hillmoor Enterprise 45392 – T.E. Moss.
Mare – Cowerslane Gem 140189 – T. Yates.
Gelding – Whitley Black Knight – Arthur Wright Farms Ltd.

1977
Stallion – Cowerslane Trueman 45588 – T. Yates.
Mare – Cowerslane Gem 140189 – T. Yates.
Gelding – Cowerslane Marty – T. Yates.

1978
Stallion – Cowerslane Trueman 45588 – T. Yates.
Mare – Cowerslane Gem 140189 – T. Yates.
Gelding – Whitley Major – A.W. Wright, Whitley Hall, Whitley, Warrington.

1979
Stallion – Cowerslane Trueman 45588 – T. Yates.
Mare – Leaphouse Pearl B459 – T. Yates.
Gelding – St Vincent's Majestic – E. Coward Ltd.

1980
Stallion – Ladbrook Aristocrat 45702 – A.W. Lewis, Little Ladbrook Farm, Tanworth in Arden, Solihull.
Mare – Jim's Lucky Charm 140492 – J.B. Cooke Ltd, 22 Halmergate, Spalding, Linconshire.
Gelding – Ty Fry Hiawatha – W.S. Innes, Ty Fry, Pentraeth, Anglesey.

1981
Stallion – Metheringham Joseph 45771 – T.E. Moss, Congleton, Cheshire
Mare – Jim's Lucky Charm 140492 – J.B. Cooke Ltd
Gelding – Cowerslane Lord – T.J. Yates, Duffield, Derby

1982
Stallion – Cubley Charlie 45853 – J. & E. Salt, The Croft, Denstone, Uttoxeter, Staffordshire.
Mare – Saredon Pure Gold 141224 – J. & E. Salt
Gelding – Cowerslane Lord – T.J. Yates

Parkington and Bisquit Cognac Shire Horse of the Year Show Champions 1974–1982

1974
Lillingstone Again (Mare) – H. Eady Robinson.
1975
Cowerslane Gem (Mare) – T. Yates.
1976
Vyrnwy Lady (Mare) – R. Livesey & Son.
1977
Cowerslane Trueman (Stallion) – T. Yates.
1978
Cowerslane Gem (Mare) – T. Yates.
1979
Jim's Lucky Charm (Mare) – J.B. Cooke Ltd.
1980
Decoy Royal Surprise (Mare) – G.T. Ward & Son Ltd.
1981
Jim's Lucky Charm (Mare) – J.B. Cooke Ltd.
1982
Jim's Lucky Charm (Mare) – J.B. Cooke Ltd.

GLOSSARY OF SHIRE HORSE TERMS

Apron   Garment worn by all drivers of turn-outs

Bevelled shoe   Slopes outwards, to make the foot appear bigger

Blaze   White marking down front of face; a lot of white is known as 'bald-headed' in the USA

Breast   Curved part of the plough that turns the furrow

Breed class   Shown to breed standards, without harness or vehicle (see **In-hand**)

By   Designates sire

Cart   Two-wheeled vehicle with shafts

Castrate   Make incapable of breeding (male)

Clean-legged   Free of long hair or feather on lower legs; Percherons and Suffolks are clean-legged breeds

Clover   Forage legume of particular value to horses; can be made into hay

Coachman   Driver of a vehicle with two or more horses

Collecting ring   Adjacent to the showing ring, where exhibits meet just before entry

Colt   Young male horse, uncastrated

Decorated class   Class where the harness and its decorations are of more consequence than the horse itself

Draught   Drawing or pulling. Also **Draft** (USA)

Dray   Four-wheeled vehicle, with seat; brewers' vehicles are usually termed drays

Driver   Person in charge of a single horse and vehicle

Dynamometer   Device for recording the pull of a horse team, without the team moving a stoneboat

Entire   Stallion

Felloes, fellies   Wooden sections of the circumference of the iron-tyred wheel

Finish   In ploughing, the place where the furrows meet from opposite directions

Filly   Young female horse, usually used in conjunction with age definition e.g. filly foal

Furrow horse   Off side horse; the right-hand one from the plough stilts; some furrow horses are trained to walk just clear of the furrow, but retain their name

Furrow wheel   Large wheel that runs in the bottom of the furrow, adjustable for width and depth

Gelding   Castrated male

Groom   In the show world, the assistant in charge of a horse, or the assistant to the coachman, riding with the vehicle

Handles   Part of the plough held by the ploughman

Headland   The end of the furrows, where the teams turn

High-cut   Unbroken furrow set on edge

Hub caps, cups   Caps which screw into the wheel centre, and are packed with grease

In-hand   Synonymous with 'breed class'; a single animal shown, usually under breed society standards

Land horse   Near side horse; the left-hand one from the plough stilts

Landside   That part of the plough which presses against the furrow wall

Land wheel   Small wheel that runs on the unploughed ground, adjustable

Mare   Female from three years onwards

Martingale   Leather strap on horse's chest, much used for decoration

Mouldboard   That part of the plough that turns the furrow over (see **Breast**)

Naff, nave   Hub of wooden wheel

Obstacle test   A race against time by turnouts through a series of markers

Open bridle   One without blinkers or blinders, so the horses can see what is behind them; those favouring the open bridle believe that the horse is less nervous when he can see the reason for any noise

Out of   Designates dam

Plough body   See **Breast**

Point, sock, share   Detachable metal point that leads the plough body into the ground. It makes the horizontal cut. Plough points became rather a fetish among ploughmen, and before 1939 an incredible range was manufactured. These were standardized to three during World War Two, and no one was worse off

Pulling contest   One or two horses pulling a loaded sledge over a certain distance, the winner continuing to do so when others have failed; the pull may also be recorded on a dynamometer

Red ticket   First prize

Ring   Area in which the animals are shown

Rulley   Four-wheeled flat-topped vehicle, usually with shafts for one horse, but no seat

Seedbed Fine, worked-down soil into which seed is drilled

Shank Rope attached to a halter's headpiece

Sledge, stoneboat Wheel-less transport used in pulling matches, of a known weight and loaded with blocks whose weights are also known

Stallion Male horse capable of breeding

Steward Judge's assistant, there to carry out his wishes and facilitate his task

Swingle tree Piece of wood or metal with hooks, joining trace chains and implement, and holding the chains apart so that they do not chafe the horses' legs

Temperament Natural disposition, e.g. fiery or placid

Trade turnout Normally applies to horses and vehicles used for deliveries or city work, not farm vehicles

Turnout Vehicle plus horse(s) in a show class; this is usually for single horse, pair, then three or four or more

Waggon Four-wheeled farm vehicle, whose style varies according to county of origin

Wagon American version of above, also used to denote a motor vehicle

BIBLIOGRAPHY

ARNOLD, JAMES, *All Drawn by Horses*, David & Charles, 1979

CARR, SAMUEL, *The Poetry of Horses*, Batsford, 1981

CHIVERS, KEITH, *The Shire Horse*, J.A. Allen, 1977, and Futura (abridged), 1978

CHIVERS/RAYNER, *The Heavy Horse Manual*, David and Charles, 1981

COCKCROFT, BARRY, *Princes of the Plough*, Dent, 1977

COSIRA, *The Blacksmith's Craft*, 1979

DENT, *Cleveland Bay Horses*, J.A. Allen, 1978

EDWARDS, LIONEL, *Horses and Ponies*, Country Life Ltd, n.d. but between 1918 and 1939

G. EWART EVANS, *Horse Power and Magic, The Pattern under the Plough, The Horse in the Furrow, The Farm and the Village, Where Beards Wag All*, and *Ask the Fellows Who Cut the Hay*, Faber, 1970s

GILBEY, SIR WALTER, Bart, *The Concise History of the Shire Horse* (reprint of the second edition), Spur Publications, Saiga Publishing Co. Ltd, Hindhead, Surrey, 1976

HART, EDWARD, *Golden Guinea Book of Heavy Horses Past and Present*, David & Charles, 1976

HART, EDWARD, *Showing Livestock*, David and Charles, 1979

HART, EDWARD, *The Heavy Horse*, Shire Publications Ltd, Princes Risborough, Bucks, 1979

HART, EDWARD, *Heavy Horses*, Batsford, 1981

HART, EDWARD, *Care and Showing of the Heavy Horse*, Batsford, 1981

HART, EDWARD, *Victorian and Edwardian Farming from old photographs*, Batsford, 1981

HENSCHEL, GEORGIE, *Horses and Ponies*, Kingfisher, 1979

JEPSEN, STANLEY, M., *The Gentle Giants, the Story of Draft Horses* (American). A.S. Barnes & Co., South Brunswick, 1971

KEEGAN, TERRY, *The Heavy Horse: Its Harness and Harness Decoration*, Pelham Books, 1973

LESSITER, FRANK, *Horse Power*, Reiman Publications, Milwaukee, Wisconsin, 1977

LLEWELLYN, JOHN, *Schoolin's Log*, Michael Joseph, 1980

NATIONAL FEDERATION OF YOUNG FARMERS' CLUBS, *Farm Horses*, 1940. Reprint 1980, Edward Hart Publications, The Yethouse, Newcastleton, Roxburghshire TD9 0TD

OAKSEY, JOHN, and LORD SNOWDON, *Pride of the Shires – the story of the Whitbread horses*, Hutchinson, 1979

TELLEEN, MAURICE, *Draft Horse Primer*, Rodale Press, 1977

THOMPSON, JOHN, *A selection of facsimiles of carts, waggons and old farm implements*, 1 Fieldway, Fleet, Hampshire

SUFFOLK HORSE SOCIETY, *The Suffolk Horse*, Church Street, Woodbridge, Suffolk, 1979

VILLIERS, GUY, *The British Heavy Horse*, Barrie & Jenkins Ltd, London, 1976

WEATHERLEY, LEE, *Heavy Horse Handbook* (booklet), Southern Counties Heavy Horse Association, 1972

WEATHERLEY, LEE, Great Horses of Britain, Saiga, 1978

WEBER and JEPSEN, *Heroes in Harness*, A.S. Barnes & Co., 1979

WHITLOCK, RALPH, *Gentle Giants*, Lutterworth Press, 1976

WRIGHT, PHILIP, A., *Salute the Cart Horse*, Ian Allen, London, 1971

INDEX

Numerals in *italic* type refer to pages on which illustrations appear